ORGANIZING
YOUR
PRAYER CLOSET

Praise for *Organizing Your Prayer Closet*

If you're a little scatterbrained like me, with your mind going six places at once, prayer can be a challenge. How do you pray? When do you pray? And what do you pray? That's why I love Gina's Prayer Closet Organizer. It's a great weapon to help me focus, be more effective, and be more intentional about listening for God's voice. Instead of wondering how I'll fill my prayer time, I'm excited about it, and you will be, too!

—Sheila Wray Gregoire, blogger at ToLoveHonorandVacuum.com

Organizing Your Prayer Closet helps you transform a cluttered prayer life into a serene sanctuary, out of which flows great power and wonderful results. Don't neglect or misplace one more prayer before committing to read Gina's book!

—Sandy Ralya, author of The Beautiful Wife curriculum, founder of Beautiful Womanhood

Gina's book will be a powerful tool in many women's lives to revitalize their relationship with God. I loved her honesty and the way she tackled some tough topics with biblical wisdom and wonderful stories.

—Dr. Sue Edwards, Associate Professor of Educational Ministries and Leadership, Dallas Theological Seminary, author of The Discover Together Bible Study series, www.discovertogetherseries.com

With the rise of professional organizers for our homes who offer hope for the chronically disorganized, I am thrilled to meet Gina Duke who offers a similar service for our life of prayer. While my closet absolutely needs help, even more so, my personal prayer life needs an overhaul. Gina Duke provides a way forward to chart our prayers, hang up our hopes, toss out our sins and laments, and then look back through the door and see the wonderful way the Holy Spirit works in our lives in due time.

—Lisa Nichols Hickman, author of *Writing in the Margins: Connecting to God on the Pages of Your Bible*

Prayer is a mysterious dialogue. Gina Duke's personal entry into this mystery serves to remove fear and infuses the reader with a sense of anticipation. *Organizing Your Prayer Closet* offers a simple, beautifully uncluttered approach to prayer. God waits to engage our hearts with conversation. We hesitate but long to be heard. Thank you, Gina, for the invitation to exhale and relax into the arms of a safe and ever present God, to hear His voice above the noise of our culture, and to find unexpected answers beyond our wildest dreams.

—Bonnie Keen, author, speaker, recording artist

GINA DUKE

ORGANIZING YOUR YOUR PRAYER CLOSET

Abingdon Press

NASHVILLE

ORGANIZING YOUR PRAYER CLOSET
A NEW AND LIFE-CHANGING WAY TO PRAY

Library of Congress Cataloging-in-Publication Data has been requested.

ISBN 978-1-4267-6895-8

16 17 18 19 20 21 22—10 9 8 7 6 5 4 3 2

MANUFACTURED IN THE UNITED STATES OF AMERICA

To my husband, Jamie:

> I love you for unconditionally loving me and allowing me to be who I am in Christ Jesus.

To my children, Kassie and Kallie:

> May you allow God to use you to your fullest potential. I love you always.

To my aunt Beverly:

> Thank you for introducing me to structured prayer journaling. Because you have always been present for all the other special milestones of my life, it is only fitting that you would be a part of this one, too.

To the FBC Portland Women:

> Stay focused on the "higher things" so you will be able to see the hand of God moving in and through your life.

CONTENTS

Introduction / 1

Chapter 1: Anchored Down / 5

Chapter 2: Praise and Thanksgiving / 15

Chapter 3: Freedom and Forgiveness / 25

Chapter 4: Prayer Petitions / 35

Chapter 5: God Answers / 45

Chapter 6: At the Right Time / 55

Chapter 7: My Heart/My Passion / 65

Chapter 8: Ambassador Notes / 75

Chapter 9: Insight and Updates / 85

Chapter 10: Ears to Hear / 95

Chapter 11: Faith and Follow-Through / 105

Notes / 115

Acknowledgments / 118

The Prayer Closet Organizer / 121

INTRODUCTION

Since high school I have loved journaling. Freehand journaling captured and clarified my thoughts, feelings, and experiences as nothing else did at the time. When I was about twenty-seven, my aunt gave me a small, leather-bound prayer journal whose page headers read "Prayer Request" and "Prayer Answer." I viewed this intriguing little book with fear and trembling. I thought, *God, who am I to keep track of You? You can do whatever You want with my prayers.* Then I thought, *Why wouldn't I record my petitions and God's answers, unless I don't think He answers them?* It was then I realized that my faith had been weak. I had not prayed expecting God to answer my prayers. I would send them up, but apparently I had no real hope of their being answered. I was just doing my prayer duty.

Have you ever felt this way about prayer? That it was merely an exercise, not a means of communicating with the God of the universe? How did this feeling affect your prayer life?

As I put this new journal to work, however, I began to see His faithfulness. How delighted I was to discover God answering prayer after prayer. I began to recognize the hand of God moving in my life, and in others' lives as I prayed for them. I saw the power in recording my requests and God's answers.

In the following years, I looked for another prayer journal just like it, but without success. Then, in 2001, the Lord taught me the concept of what I am about to share with you: the Prayer Closet Organizer. In this day and time, we spend small fortunes on time management planners and electronic devices, and numerous hours updating our calendars to keep track of our worldly lives. So why wouldn't we take the same time and commitment to get a handle on our spiritual lives?

The Prayer Closet Organizer is a journaling method that will enable you to:

- Offer meaningful worship.
- Spiritually grow by overcoming sin.
- Hear God with clarity.
- Discover the wonderful, God-inspired story that the Lord is working through you.
- Experience the pleasure of obedience to God's will.
- Become a proactive ambassador of Christ.
- Discern God's calling for your life.
- Remember prayer requests.
- Learn how to pray with Scripture.
- Record how God is using you to affect the lives of others.
- Develop faith and confidence in the sovereignty of God.

In a nutshell, the Prayer Closet Organizer will train you to focus on the higher things of God. Your prayer life will become everything God intended, and as your faith grows, you will become the Christian God intended.

How the Organizer Makes a Difference

The Prayer Closet Organizer is an effective resource for clear-minded, disciplined prayer. Each section of the organizer is specifically designed to meet both practical and reflective needs of prayer.

This tool offers you a private escape into the presence of God for some meaningful one-on-one time. Jesus Himself often went to private places to spend time alone with God. The Son of God had a habit of retreating for prayer to a garden, a mountain, and a boat. He regularly escaped to solitary places despite His hectic and demanding ministry and travels. In fact, He told us to do the same thing—and promised to bless us for doing so: "When thou prayest, enter into thy closet, and when thou hast shut thy door, pray to thy Father which is in secret; and thy Father which seeth in secret shall reward thee openly" (Matthew 6:6 KJV).

The book in your hand is your new solitary place for prayer. The Prayer Closet Organizer can be used anytime and anywhere. Whether you are in a busy waiting room or at a noisy soccer game, you can enter into your prayer closet for a moment of solitude and comforting conversation with God.

Get ready to enter into your prayer closet—a place prepared for you. A place to sort your thoughts before you enter into a time of prayer. Before the conversation with God can begin, you will want to gather your thoughts, search for your words, and make sure you bring every needful thing before Jesus. Your time is precious. The people in your life are important. Your prayer requests are special. Throughout the day, you uncover one thing at a time that needs to be brought before the Lord. Maybe you have a friend with an illness, a neighbor with a troubled marriage, or a child who is struggling. You can carry their needs to God in your Prayer Closet Organizer.

In this guide, I will help you organize your prayer closet, one section at a time. Picture in your mind's eye a wardrobe armoire with a rod, shelves, and drawers. A structured and well-thought-out prayer closet promises no muddled thoughts or frantic searching for words. In your organizer you can put your thoughts in order, take them confidently to the Lord, and see His love in His answers.

Are you ready for a transformed prayer life? Are you ready to see God at work? Are you excited to fulfill your purpose as God's child?

Enter in!

Pray with your intelligence.
Bring things to God that you have
thought out and think them out again with Him.
That is the secret of good judgment.
—Charles H. Brent[1]

Author's Note:

The names and identifying details of a few of the people in these pages have been changed.[2]

CHAPTER 1
ANCHORED DOWN

The end of everything has come. Therefore, be self-controlled
and clearheaded so you can pray.
—1 Peter 4:7

I've been writing weekly prayer tips on my blog since 2012. As I was recently preparing to write another, I took a pause, as I felt like I had written everything that could possibly be written about the precious topic of prayer. But, lo and behold, the Holy Spirit assured me that the topic of prayer was as infinite as the topic of God. Since prayer is attached to the

Eternal One, its breadth and depth are as limitless as He is. With a sigh of relief, I continued typing away on my keyboard.

If you are wondering how I am unearthing all my weekly prayer points, I will tell you—Scripture. Tucked away in many of the holy passages are little treasures of prayer instruction. Take Psalm 100:4 for example:

> Enter his gates with thanks;
> enter his courtyards with praise!
> Thank him! Bless his name!

See the instruction? If we want to enter into His gates, we do so with thanksgiving by expressing thanks to Him. In order to enter into His courts, we come with praise, which is expressed when we bless His Name. Have you blessed His Name lately? This is not something we hear or even talk a lot about, is it? We may say, "We bless Your name, Lord!" but I don't think that is what He is after.

According to the instruction of this Scripture, when I receive healing from an ailment, I should respond by simply saying, "Thank You, Lord, for healing me," followed by, "I bless Your Name Jehovah-Rophi," which means "The Lord who heals."

Another reason I am compelled to do this is because I am convinced that "gates" and "courts" are two separate destinations. The thanksgiving that gets me through the gates places me on holy ground, but blessing His name gets me into my King's court—into His divine presence.

See how one little verse can open up a whole new view of the power of prayer? That is why Scripture is my go-to for prayerful insight. One of my favorite things to do in my Prayer Closet Organizer is to review all of my praises for the week and then sum them up with a divine title of the Holy Trinity that best describes my entries. Then, I bless His name in my time of prayer.

I felt equally excited when I came upon 1 Peter 4:7: "The end of everything has come. Therefore, be self-controlled and clearheaded so you can pray."

If you are like me, you may be prone to skip over this verse once you begin reading, "the end of everything has come" because it has an end-times tone to it. But reconsider so you don't miss out on the point that Peter is trying to make. Peter is simply interjecting a sense of urgency into our prayer lives. As soon as I catch wind that friends are having marital problems, I begin praying immediately. It would not be wise for me to start praying when the issue is confirmed by a divorce filing. Agree?

A House of Mourning

The second instruction from 1 Peter 4:7 is to be serious. That's easy, right? I think we all recognize that prayer is a serious matter and that we should be serious about prayer. But does our seriousness match the kind of seriousness that Peter is encouraging?

You see, the kind of seriousness that Peter is talking about is the same kind of seriousness that King Solomon was speaking of when he said, "It is better to go to a house of mourning / than to go to a house of feasting" (Ecclesiastes 7:2 NIV). Really? I mean, who in their right mind would rather spend the evening grieving the death of a loved one at the funeral home instead of getting together with friends for a party, with food?

In Solomon's God-given wisdom, he understood people. He understood that we live toward a house of feasting. We have a mentality that looks forward to things like new movie releases, vacation destinations, and home renovation projects. We live for the running, doing, and playing for the majority of our lives, don't we? I know I do, and I certainly know my kids do, too!

I can remember one Christmas when we finished unwrapping Christmas gifts and my daughters asked about our vacation plans for the next summer.

And I'll have to admit that I was just as excited to hear my husband's thoughts on the subject.

But you see, a house of mourning experience unspoils us from the house of feasting mentality. When we are at the funeral home, we become much more serious about the important things in life. We begin to focus on others and less on ourselves. We contemplate eternal things in those moments. These moments are critical for our spiritual temperament despite how much we despise and dread them. It is in these moments we become solemnly serious, and that is the very disposition Peter advises we take into prayer.

When I use the enclosed Prayer Closet Organizer during a formal time of prayer, I like to start off with thanksgiving and praise as I have described. I follow that with a time of reflection and repentance about my failings. But before I begin to rattle off my prayer requests, I go to my house of mourning.

I feel called to intercede for abused and neglected children despite the fact that I feel called to women's ministry. I am not sure why this is, but this very sad reality vexes my soul, and I become solemnly serious. That is where I start praying over my listed prayer needs. It brings a serious authenticity to my prayer requests. Once I finish praying for these children, I go to the petitions on my list with the same solemn attitude.

A couple of years ago, there were two little twin boys in foster care with a family at our church. Immediately, I was drawn to them and loved them as if they were my own. They were the cutest boys and since my husband is also a twin, we were drawn to them immediately. I had hoped to adopt them but needed confirmation that it was God's will. My husband and I took them on little dates to a dinosaur exhibition and additional field trips to get to know them better. After a couple of outings, they were gone. Their parent's rights had just been severed and the government agency moved them from our friend's foster home to an adoptive home. There was nothing we could do, as we had no rights to them. It devastated me. Now, my house of mourning is the faces of two little seven-year-old twin boys. They remind me that my prayers are precious and deserve more than honorable mentions.

Sometimes my house of mourning is a burden I am carrying for someone. Other times it may be something serious on the world stage that has struck a chord deep inside me. Although, my house of mourning changes depending on the felt need of the moment, my home of mourning remains abused and neglected children. What would you say is your main house of mourning?

Watch unto Prayer

The last point Peter makes in 1 Peter 4:7 is to be disciplined for prayer. Statistics show that a third of Christians are dissatisfied with their prayer lives. I find it odd that the essence of prayer—whispers to God anytime and anywhere—is so easy; yet, by and large, it seems to be the most difficult discipline to maintain.

For many years I would set a time of prayer aside for when I got into bed, like most folks do. While my intentions were good, my body disagreed, as it would fall to sleep during my prayer time. My problem was that everything I was doing leading up to going to bed was telling my body that it was about to go to sleep. I would put on the most comfortable big T-shirt and equally comfy flannel pants, lay down on my soft mattress and favorite pillow, and cover myself with the warm covers—oh, I am yawning even now! This is one of the things that I love about structured prayer journaling—it keeps me awake for prayer.

If you were to look up the various translations for 1 Peter 4:7, you would see the many different ways it translates this particular verse. This Scripture not only ends with "self-controlled and clearheaded so you can pray" but also *The Message* translation says to, "Stay wide-awake in prayer." I find it fascinating that Peter is begging us to stay awake to pray when he fell asleep not only once or twice, but three times in the Garden of Gethsemane. Maybe he has since learned a thing or two?

Do you not notice when your husband or coworker is in a concerning mood even though they have not mentioned anything bothersome? You just know because of the amount of time you spend with them; you can tell something is off. I can hardly believe that Peter did not have that same feeling with Jesus that night. Jesus, the disciples' go-to guy, was requesting they pray because He was so overwhelmed with sadness He felt like dying (see Matthew 26:38). I don't know why their ears didn't perk up at such words from the One who calmed storms and cast out demons. Case in point: if it is that easy for Peter to fall asleep despite Jesus's plea, how much more are we prone to fall asleep during prayer?

The two other most cited translations for "disciplined in prayer" is to be "sober" and another one of my favorites, "watch unto prayer." As I journal prayers in my Prayer Closet Organizer, I am watching God answer them. I am watching how and when He answers them. Sometimes the hardest things to capture are answered prayers because, as you know, answered prayers are not instantaneous.

The Waiting Game

Structured prayer journaling requires me to wait and watch. From my own personal experience, I have discovered that God is either taking me *through* something or *to* something. And it is those two scenarios that set my eyes toward the two faces of hope. Depending on whether or not God is taking me *to* something or *through* something will determine which face I will seek.

Last year, I returned to a full-time career as a Human Resources and Safety Manager in order to get my younger daughter through college debt-free. This meant that I left full-time ministry work where I would spend the week in my pajamas on my couch blogging and writing. Soon after returning to the workforce, my mother was diagnosed with a benign brain tumor, but the surgery left her in hospice care. These two things have rocked my world to say the least. I have been not only shocked back into fifty- to sixty-hour workweeks and trying to ensure my mother's care but also trying to continue writing at the same pace in order to fulfill obligations. Let me tell you that God has been faithfully taking me through this season of difficulty and great sadness, but not without some stumbles on my part.

As my troubled year was winding down, my husband planned a getaway for much needed rest and time together. As the vacation neared, I began to allow this little hiatus from life to become my lifeline to surviving the hard days and weeks leading up to it. I would often say something like, "Just six more weeks" and "If I can just make it to the second week of November!" But the Lord wasn't having it.

I felt His conviction over my faith that had been misplaced in this second honeymoon to get me through difficult days. It was like He was warning me not to depend upon that house-of-feasting mentality but to rely on Him; a house of feasting will always leave us wanting more. This reminded me of Hebrews 6:19, which says, "We have this hope as an anchor for the soul, firm and secure. It enters the inner sanctuary behind the curtain" (NIV). My Heavenly Father was beckoning me to come into the Holy of Holies with my hope in Him. That is what prayer journaling does for me; it allows me to stop and ponder what I have written against the reality of my inclinations and the hope of His truth. Now, as God brings me through this sad season, my eyes are set on the face of the Anchor of my soul.

The other face of hope is that of the wings of an eagle. Has God ever given you a divine peak? Perhaps it is a seed He has planted for ministry or direction for the use of a spiritual gift. Maybe it is something of a side business that you love the idea of. Whatever it may be, it places you on a path where God is leading you to something.

I've been on such a road for many years in ministry. It has had ups and downs, exciting times and quiet times, exuberant moments and frustrating ones for sure. It is because of the lulls and valley visits that I had never cared for Isaiah 40:31, which goes on and on about soaring with wings like an eagle. If I am honest, I probably have rolled my eyes at this Scripture a time or two. When I think of an eagle soaring, I see an eagle who has already arrived at the desired elevation point and is enjoying his flight. That picture has not been representative of my journey in ministry.

As I was pondering this Scripture, as I often do others I do not particularly mesh with, I realized that in some translations, it instead uses the words "mount up." In particular it says, "They that wait upon the Lord shall renew their strength; they shall mount up with wings as eagles; they shall run, and not be weary; and they shall walk, and not faint" (KJV). I had often viewed the mounting up as a result of good waiting, which I have never been particularly good at; but now I view this differently. Those who wait well do these things: renew their strength, mount up, run and do not get weary, walk and not faint. These are the things we do while we wait on the Lord, trust in the Lord, and hope in the Lord!

As I follow after God and His plan for my life, I look toward the face of hope that resembles the wings of an eagle and I mount up. I'll never forget all the years I studied, wrote, and archived messages for an audience of women I did not have. I often reminded God of this reality but thanked Him anyway for the things that He stirred in my heart. And today, I am glad I did the mounting up preparation so that when He gave me an opportunity, I was ready for launch. Maybe you are in that place, too?

Whatever your life may hold, I pray it will be bathed in prayer. The next few chapters hold prayerful insight and tips for effectual prayer. It is my pleasure to share peeks into my prayer closet with you.

Organizing Your Prayer Closet

When I sit down at the end of the day, I grab my copy of *Organizing Your Prayer Closet* for some prayer journaling time. I make new entries and update old ones; this is how I organize my prayer closet. How will you organize yours? Consider the following:

- Have you reviewed the structured prayer journal, *The Prayer Closet Organizer*, beginning on page 110?
- Do you plan to prayer journal in the morning, evening, or throughout the day?
- Is there a place in your home that you like to use for prayer?
- Have you thought about using some other additions that may enhance your journaling experience like a good pen or decorative washi tape and stickers?

Let me pray for you.

Dear Alpha and Omega, I bless Your name! I pray for my new friend, who is about to begin the new experience of structured prayer journaling. May You further reveal Yourself in every page, every tip, every entry, and every answered prayer. And when this journal is complete, I pray that my friend will be amazed at all You have done. All glory to You!

It is godly [people] who give over themselves entirely to prayer. Prayer is far-reaching in its influence and in its gracious effects. It is intense and profound business which deals with God and His plans and purposes, and it takes whole-hearted [people] to do it. No half-hearted, half-brained, half-spirited effort will do for this serious, all-important, heavenly

*business. The whole heart, the whole brain,
the whole spirit, must be in the matter of
praying, which is so mightily to affect the
characters and destinies of [those who pray].*
    —E. M. Bounds, The Essentials of Prayer[1]

CHAPTER 2
PRAISE AND THANKSGIVING

Shout triumphantly to the Lord, all the earth!
Serve the Lord with celebration!
Come before him with shouts of joy!
Know that the Lord is God—
he made us; we belong to him.
We are his people,
the sheep of his own pasture.
Enter his gates with thanks;
enter his courtyards with praise!
Thank him! Bless his name!

Because the LORD *is good,*

his loyal love lasts forever;

his faithfulness lasts generation after generation.

—*Psalm 100*

P rayer should always begin with praise and thanksgiving. Psalm 100 tells us to "enter his gates with thanks; / enter his courtyards with praise! / Thank him! Bless his name!" (v. 4). As you begin to organize your prayer closet, survey your day to recount the things you want to honor God for in praise. It may be that you received a kind word from a coworker, or you realized at some point during your day that God's presence was evident in a particular situation. Thanksgiving brings a humble posture to prayer. In reflection on God's blessings and many provisions, a thankful heart is appropriate.

In church, have you ever noticed that sometimes there is an awkward silence just before a congregational prayer? It usually follows the question, "Does anyone have a praise to report?" There are always plenty of prayer requests, but typically few praises. Unfortunately, I think this may be the norm in a lot of churches. I'm always upset when no one, including myself, can think of even one good, noteworthy thing God has done lately. It is incredible. God is definitely doing great things in my life, but with the everyday hustle and bustle and a multitude of distractions, it is hard to get a clear thought for an appropriate response to that question.

Since I began journaling my praises along with those things I am thankful for, I can more readily give an account of God's goodness. The department of Praise and Thanksgiving is the first area to review as you begin to organize your prayer closet before a formal time of prayer. Praise and thanksgiving are the segue into God's presence.

Praise = Presence

Psalm 22:3 states, "But thou art holy, O thou that inhabitest the praises of Israel" (KJV). This gives me a marvelous word picture of God's presence resting above the voices of a worshiping congregation—or a worshiping individual. And when I can feel God's presence in such a manner it is incomparable to anything joyful, exciting, or awesome this world can offer. To feel as if I am truly standing near God is something I seek!

You and I live in a rough world where people are randomly killed in movie theaters, spouses are abandoned, and children are abused by their parents. To have a moment where I can feel engulfed by God's presence and escape into the heavenlies for a divinely imposed break is priceless to me.

With some creative license I'd like to stretch Psalm 22:3 into another connotation by rephrasing it this way: *The more I praise and thank God, the more I will experience God's presence in my life.* This thought raises the value of worship. There have been times when I have desperately cried out to God to feel His presence in my life, times when I felt distant, disconnected, and full of worry. Scripture says to "come near to God, and he will come near to you" (James 4:8). One way I know to come near to God during these difficult times is through praise. Maybe this is why we are taught by Jesus Himself in the Lord's Prayer to start with praise, so that God's presence will come close (Matthew 6:9-13).

In the human experience of checking off lists and climbing the corporate ladder, it is valuable for me to acknowledge that God is also working on my behalf in ways I cannot always see. This understanding reassures me that I am loved and cared for in a tremendous way, no matter how things may appear. As I capture those moments in my day where God has divinely interjected Himself, I am reminded that my life is about something more than to-do lists and personal success. For me worship is a place to pause and admire the one Person who can never fail me and loves me unconditionally.

When Praise Seems Elusive

Whenever I am having trouble beginning my time of prayer with praise, I ask myself the same question Jesus asked in Matthew 22:42: "What do you think about the Christ? Whose son is he?"

Your answer to this question might surprise you. Think about it—who is Jesus to you? I was surprised by my own revelations as I stewed over this question.

The Pharisees who surrounded Jesus that day answered Him, "The son of David" (v. 42). Jesus being a son of David held special meaning to the Jews, just as Jesus' personal meaning to us individually can be just as special. For me, it all started with a friend with whom I was working on a ministry project. Her constant dialogue about Jesus stood out to me. I considered myself a pretty radical follower of Christ, but there was something about her real, ongoing love affair with Jesus that disturbed me. Why?

Because I realized I wasn't sure I felt the same way about Jesus. I had received salvation, but from listening to my friend, I became keenly aware that something was not right on my end. So, I did what most of us do when we become uncomfortable with a confronting subject—I shelved it. Some time later the Holy Spirit confronted me with the pointed question from Matthew 22:42; it was as if the Spirit was demanding, "Gina, what do you think about the Christ?" The question was so convicting that I was startled by its intensity. Over the next few months, this question stayed with me, and I began to hash out my thoughts during my daily commute to work.

This wonderful question led me through a beautiful journey of thought and reflection. Over the years, between the time I "shelved" my inferior thoughts about Jesus and the Spirit's nudging me to answer the question, I had seen good times and bad, ups and downs—but Jesus had seen me through all of them. While I've never experienced a real tragedy, I can identify with the brokenhearted. I have had a couple of good blows to the heart that I was sure would do me in, but for Jesus. So as I thought about what Christ meant to me, I knew one thing—Jesus was the Lover of my soul. I'd learned that whatever my emotional need may have been, Jesus could fill it. With Jesus as the Lover of my soul, I know there will never be a day when I am not good or pretty enough for Him. I never have to worry that He is going to leave me. His love is complete; there is nothing lacking. I am confident in His love. Yes, Jesus is the Lover of my soul! It is from the deep places in our hearts that our authentic praise comes forth. From an emotional standpoint, what do you think about the Christ?

This thought-provoking question of Matthew 22:42 has been transformational in my praise and worship experience, to say the least. I once did not know how to start my prayers, but by answering this simple question, I can now quickly enter into an authentic time of praise and thanksgiving, giving Jesus the honor He deserves and God expects. This question was once overwhelming to me, but now every time I think about it, it draws a smile to my face. I am reminded of just how wonderful Jesus is. So allow me to ask you this: what do you think about the Christ? Can you embrace Jesus in such a way to allow Him to meet your needs? Maybe Jesus is your Healer, Strong Tower, Friend, or Provider. Whatever He has become to you, praise Him as you enter prayer.

Why "Boring" Is Good

In 2000, my husband of less than one year, Jamie, almost died from a sudden illness produced by an atypical strand of pneumonia. Prior to his illness, I had been in a rut. Every morning on my way to work, I was filled with dread and complaint. But for the fifteen days I spent at the hospital as my dearly beloved's life hung in the balance, I would have gladly driven that stretch of interstate headed to work as if it were any boring old day. That experience of watching my loved one suffer taught me to love "boring." A day of my normal comings and goings without the unwanted interruption of bad news is the kind of day for which I am thankful. It means all is well.

In moments when I am tempted to digress to that place of dissatisfaction, I remember those long days and nights of camping out in a waiting room full of strangers, while my husband lay unconscious in the Intensive Care Unit. Troubles of sickness, loss, and disappointment distract us momentarily from the running, working, and playing we do for the majority of our lives. Those dreadful moments teach us to be thankful when all is as it should be.

Although happy moments readily come to mind when I am viewing this section of the Prayer Closet Organizer, the very base of my gratefulness rests in the days where I am simply thankful that I can pay my bills, have dinner with my family, and enjoy the day I have planned, even if it is not very "interesting." Valuing ho-hum—because it indicates the absence of deep difficulty—has fostered a life of contentment. And when I am content with my life, I am not longing for something else bigger, better, or newer. Thanksgiving is like a comforting blanket of protection over my life.

When I am discontent with what I have or with my lot in life and begin to live in want of pointless things, I am prone to have a black, thankless heart. Paul wrote, "Obscene language, silly talk, or vulgar jokes aren't acceptable for believers. Instead, there should be thanksgiving" (Ephesians 5:4). May my lips be disciplined by the words of thanksgiving. I have often thought it would be a good experiment to try phrasing all my words in the context of a thanksgiving. Would I be less prone to complain about someone if I am sharing my gratitude for that person with another? I think so.

Thanksgiving Is a Safeguard

Thanksgiving is a great antidote to spiritual atrophy in word, thought, and deed. After realizing how many times thanksgiving is strategically placed in Scripture, I began to place more emphasis on being thankful during my prayer time. Romans 1:21 states that because people did not honor or thank God "their reasoning became pointless, and their foolish hearts were darkened." In response to this Scripture I particularly like to try to be thankful for the very thing I want to complain about. That is where the real, true seed of thanksgiving is cultivated. If I am able to thank God only during the good days, then my posture of gratitude is not truly grounded.

I like to spend money; if you don't believe me, just ask my husband. He is apt to show you the pie chart of my monthly spending habits that he often shares with me when we have the "money talk." Thanks to his "encouragement," I am doing much better. Still, my husband continually keeps me in check. As you might guess, I am prone to complain that I can't buy everything I want. I currently have seven different "dream home" boards on Pinterest, not to mention the ones I have for restoring furniture, remodeling, and redecorating, plus ones for dream vacations and must-have stylish clothes. I have actually found Pinterest to be very therapeutic for facilitating fake spending sprees, but when I get to that place where I am really unhappy about the clothes in my closet or the outdated look of my kitchen cabinets, I know that I must reframe my thoughts under the calming influence of thankfulness.

Years ago, my elder daughter, a senior in high school, announced that she was pregnant. Today, she and her husband have two beautiful little boys, a lovely home, a solid marriage, and are serving Jesus; the enemy underestimated the power of my God. Still, I will admit that the first few months after finding out about my daughter's pregnancy were difficult. My response? I kept thanking God for various things about my daughter. On a regular basis, out loud, I thanked God she wasn't sick, addicted to drugs, missing, or spiritually lost. My husband would ask me why I kept saying these things, and I would answer, "Because whatever is going on, it can always be worse." That was how I kept my situation in perspective. Nothing comes to me that has not been allowed by God. God is sovereign, so even when the hard days come, I want to be thankful. Do you currently have a situation in which you need to think of some thankful thoughts?

I encourage you to resist the temptation to gloss over this section of your Prayer Closet Organizer. Praise and thanksgiving will reframe your thoughts and draw God near.

Organizing Your Prayer Closet

Take a few moments and ponder the following, then fill in the lines on your Prayer Closet Organizer worksheet.

- What is my praise for the Lord today?
- What am I especially thankful for today?
- What good thing has happened today for which I want give God glory and honor?
- What unpleasant thing has happened today to which I want to attach thankful thoughts?

Some of my examples are:

PRAISE & THANKSGIVING
What may I praise and
thank God for today?

"Bless the Lord! The God of our salvation
supports us day after day!"
—Psalm 68:19

Jana's pregnancy despite fertility issues
400 souls saved during our mission trip!
Lindsey accepted my invite to church!
Thankful for my job despite the long hours

22

As I enter into my prayer time with the Prayer Closet Organizer, I take the Scripture in the header (each section of the Prayer Closet Organizer has a correlating Scripture in the header) and speak it to God in my prayer of specific praises and thanksgiving.

"Bless the Lord! / The God of our salvation supports us day after day!" (Psalm 68:19). Heavenly Father, I come before You with praise and thanksgiving, exalting Your Son, Jesus, the Lover of my soul. Thank You for Your goodness and mercy, and the truth of Psalm 68:19. I am thrilled for Jana and give You glory for blessing her with this baby. I am overwhelmed with joy because of all of those precious souls who received salvation during the Honduran mission trip; I am confident there is rejoicing in heaven as well. I thank You for the spiritual progress being made in Lindsey's life right now. May she continue to be drawn to You through God's people at church. Thank You for leading me to my new job. Even though the hours are long, I am at peace in knowing You have placed me there. Thank You for Your continual leading in my life; You make all the difference. I praise You and I thank You!

Yes, *worship of the loving God
is man's whole reason for existence.*
—A. W. Tozer[1]

CHAPTER 3
FREEDOM AND
FORGIVENESS

This is what we know: the person that we used to be was crucified with Him in order to get rid of the corpse that had been controlled by sin. That way we wouldn't be slaves to sin anymore, because a person who has died has been freed from sin's power.

—Romans 6:6-7

Why care about sin? For one, God will not be able to use me to His fullest extent if I am continually living as a sinner. Moreover, I will never grow into a mature Christian. We must be attuned to our spiritual imperfections.

I mentioned in chapter 1 the time my husband, Jamie, became deathly ill. That illness occurred because he had been ignoring his body's warnings. Despite a nagging cough and his inability to sleep at night, he kept working, traveling, and treating his symptoms with allergy medicine. He kept on this way until he landed in the Intensive Care Unit. His mother, a nurse, said that he must have been out of touch with his body and unable to recognize what turned out to be a dangerous, life-threatening illness.

And so it is with many of us, when we become out of touch with our flesh and the sickness of sin spreads to destroy our spiritual health. We may be going through all the motions of obedience by attending every church service or volunteering for every good initiative as expected, and still we may be ignoring some important symptoms.

Freedom is a word we can all truly love and appreciate. Because of Jesus' death on the cross, we no longer have to live in bondage to the sins of our flesh or as victims of the enemy. God wants more for us than we even want for ourselves. Second Corinthians 5:17 says that I am a "new creation" in Christ Jesus. I am different now, from who I used to be and from this world. God has set my feet on a new path where I desire to be more like Jesus. If I am freed from sin, I cannot be content to act like my old self. I want to be diligent in my process of becoming more like Jesus, more like the person God wants to me to be.

Paul wrote,

> *Now set aside these things, such as anger, rage, malice, slander, and obscene language. Don't lie to each other. Take off the old human nature with its practices and put on the new nature, which is renewed in knowledge by conforming to the image of the one who created it. (Colossians 3:8-10)*

At some point, we all have to deal with our junk. So let's get started. When I look at my issues, I see a sometimes loose tongue, overactive bouts of self-centeredness, and some lingering memories of schoolgirl regrets that tend to set me back. Most of us go through our days without realizing what we are displaying to the world. We are not aware of our actions and reactions and how they can bring a reproach to the name of Christ and the local body of believers with whom we serve. We must look at our issues, and bring them before the Lord, our Healer and Deliverer. I did not become a Christian just so I can stay tripped up in sin! Neither did you. Here is where the Prayer Closet Organizer comes in handy.

It Serves as a Mirror

As I began prayer journaling, I felt led to review my shortcomings and sins for each day. I began writing my issues down. Today, using this honest mirror, I long to humbly acknowledge these issues before the Lord, to be truly sorrowful. I won't practice self-condemnation or take on guilt, but I will recognize my failings so I can mature spiritually. I have the blessed assurance of my salvation, yet I desire to live a Spirit-led, Spirit-controlled life for His honor and His glory. And I cannot do that without walking in freedom from sin.

I never look at these issues and think, *This is who I am.* These sins happen when I do not allow Jesus Christ to reign supreme in my life. As believers we are the righteousness of God, but the world may not be seeing that in us. While this is not a plea to be perfect in our own strength, it is a reminder to surrender our issues to the One who can set us free.

Our issues take on various forms. Some come from past hurts, insecurities, physical and emotional abuse, emotional immaturity, and sometimes just plain old bad decision making. Wherever we have picked up these habits, the prayer closet is the place to begin undoing them.

As I work with my prayer organizer, I think about what I have done that day that gave me the terrible feeling of conviction. I recall any time I failed to do something I should have done, such as tell someone about Jesus when given the opportunity. It is important that we assess our issues of spiritual weakness; as we faithfully fill out the Freedom and Forgiveness section of our Prayer Closet Organizers, we recognize patterns and see what sins continually beset us.

The Battle Begins

It was after a few months of prayer journaling that I decided to go back and review my entries. I looked at every category and made updates. The last department I checked was the one on Freedom and Forgiveness, and I was surprised by what I learned about myself.

I am a repeat offender! No telling how many times I acknowledged the same issues with my tongue, pride, and some other not-so-nice issues. God had revealed to me that I had behavior patterns that were not going down without a fight, and this was going to be one battle that I had to take on if I wanted to grow: the battle with myself.

Are you aware of some recurring bad behaviors? Do you find yourself continually asking forgiveness for the same things? See if my plan of attack would be helpful for you.

After some thought and prayer, I knew that my best weapon was going to be the Word of God. So, with my newfound issues clearly defined for me, I began to scour the Scriptures. Did you know that Scripture addresses just about every type of sin we may have? Nothing gets past God. Not only did I find verses galore about the words we speak, but for every kind of pride and other issues.

It was time for a spiritual tongue-piercing, if you will. My problems ranged from gossiping and lack of discretion to harsh words and loud-mouthed, attention-getting shenanigans. It was completely out of control! Thank the Lord I found a gem of a Scripture that not only helped tame my tongue, it also addressed all of my other bad habits. I refer back to it time and again when I am beginning to feel spiritually undisciplined: "We all stumble in many ways. Anyone who is never at fault in what they say is perfect, able to keep their whole body in check" (James 3:2 NIV).

Do you see what this means? It means that we all sin in various ways, but if we are able to discipline our speech, then we will be able to bring our whole body under control. This is a one-size-fits-all, no-matter-what-kind-of-sin-you've-got-you-can-break-free verse! This is truth. God's Word also says, "The tongue is a small flame of fire, a world of evil at work in us. It contaminates our entire lives. Because of it, the circle of life is set on fire. The tongue itself is set on fire by the flames of hell" (James 3:6). In case I had been thinking that my untamed tongue was not a problem, I had to think again. It may have been the very place where all my issues started. And I needed to battle my bad habits just as I would use a good weed killer: I had to start at the root—my mouth.

After latching onto this jewel of James 3:2, I made it a priority to begin praying this Scripture and my specially selected Scriptures over myself every day during my commute to work. And guess what happened? I immediately began to feel a more Spirit-controlled temperament in this flesh of mine. I started catching myself before uttering some unhelpful words. Before I made hurtful remarks, I thought about this Scripture and my personal commitment to be more Spirit-disciplined. You will have to try it to experience the same influence of commitment and steadfastness.

The Toughest Sin of All

Although I experienced much progress in this area, I still had one issue that was holding on for dear life. As transparent as I like to be, this is one issue I do not want to reveal. You may even have one of your own: a habit that brings not only sin but shame. You can't even talk about it.

I couldn't write this one down in my prayer journal; I wouldn't even know what to call it. Sometimes there just aren't any names to assign to our craziness. So just to be safe with my secret, whenever this issue reared its ugly little head, I would note it in my Prayer Closet Organizer in the Freedom and Forgiveness section by drawing a frowny face. Over and over, it left me overridden with feelings of guilt. My frowny-face sin was hindering me from living an abundant life; it had to go.

So again I searched the Scriptures for its perfect anecdote and continued to pray verses over myself every day—for three years. (I never said this was going to be quick and easy! Sometimes dealing with sinful habits is a slow process of undoing years of damage.) I would go for a period of time with great success, and then a setback would occur, but I would not be deterred. I knew that God's Word could break the hold this sin had on me, and I was committed to the plan I felt the Holy Spirit gave me.

Then one day I was released! While on my commute, praying over this issue, I felt God ask me a question: "Gina, how long has it been since you have succumbed to this sin?" I couldn't even recall how long it had been, but I understood what God was really saying: "You are free from this." As soon as I got home that day, I went to my Prayer Closet Organizer to look up my last frowny-face entry. It had been almost five months since I noted this sin, and I knew that it no longer ruled me. The best part about this happy ending was that God had announced my freedom Himself with His question.

The Bottom Line

Nothing hinders prayer like sin, unforgiveness, or rebellion. We may be the righteousness of God, but we still live in this bothersome tent of flesh. It trips us up, binds us, and likes to draw us away from our heavenly Father. We develop bad habits and live haphazardly. All of these things interfere with healthy Christian living and an effective prayer life.

If you are inclined to skip over this department in your Prayer Closet Organizer, I want to caution you that your shortcut may cost you your spiritual maturity, not to mention the witness you want to be to others. Without a doubt, this is where I have experienced the most spiritual growth in my journey of faith. As a young Christian, I used to be amazed at church leaders who lost their effectiveness and opportunity in ministry because of the trap of sin. I have found that if you are serious about your spiritual growth, Satan will get just as serious—in a different direction. We must be on guard. John 10:10 tells us that the enemy has come to kill, steal, and destroy. He is going for the death blow, and we must be aware of our issues in order to arm ourselves for Satan's well-planned attack.

Accountability seems to be in vogue these days because people and ministries realize that without it, they are prone to be deceived. Sometimes it can be hard to find the right person to be one's accountability partner or to find the time for an accountability session, so this department is the next best thing, as well as a good place to start.

As we daily consider where we missed the mark, we recognize our continual need for God. Without Jesus reigning in our hearts, we are left to our own devices. We have bad habits that need correcting, and renewal starts with acknowledging our issues. The good news is that God has forgiven us and set us free from all sin.

Organizing Your Prayer Closet

As you sit before the Lord today, review the following questions and record the answers in your organizer:

- Can I recall any moment today where I clearly know that I sinned?
- Did I feel convicted by the Holy Spirit over any of my actions today?
- Do I have any bad habits that need correction?

- What things did I fail to do?
- Has the Holy Spirit revealed any stubborn sins in my life?

Some of my examples have been:

FREEDOM & FORGIVENESS
What am I
struggling with?

*"Then Jesus said to her,
'Your sins are forgiven.' "*
—Luke 7:48

* *Ignored You when prompted to witness to Cindy*
* *Made negative comments at work*
* *Speaking too harshly to my girls lately*
* *Procrastination and laziness this week*

The goal here is to take these confessions into our Prayer Closet Organizer and ask God to help us do better. Be sure to include the Scripture in your prayer, as I have here:

Lord, I am encouraged that my sins are forgiven. And because of this great truth, may I never again delay in sharing the gospel with someone whom You are prompting me to witness to. Please forgive me; I pray for another opportunity. The truth is that I have a hope in Jesus Christ and should be a positive reflection of that hope. May I concentrate on Your goodness and focus less on the irritating things I deal with at work. God, I do not want always to be fussing at my girls. I want to be a mother who responds with loving correction when needed and soft words of love and understanding. May I make them a priority and not treat them as a distraction or interruption.

Lord, I have so many things that need to be done, and although I know it is healthy to take a mental break and have some physical rest, I do not want them to dominate my time, especially when I have project work to accomplish and responsibilities to uphold. Help me to be disciplined and committed to the tasks at hand. Thank You, Lord, for Your assistance in helping me with my daily life.

Above all the grace and the gifts that Christ gives to his beloved is that of overcoming self.
—Francis of Assisi[1]

CHAPTER 4
PRAYER PETITIONS

The LORD has listened to my request.
The LORD accepts my prayer.
—Psalm 6:9

Now we get to the part of prayer that most think is the *only* reason we pray. Don't misunderstand; petitions are vitally important, but far from the only reason to pray.

As we focus on this aspect of our organizer, I must share a shameful scene from someone's past; dare I disclose it to be mine? My friend Lynn called one night to give me an update regarding the serious health condition of her father. I had committed to pray for her dad. This would have been a great picture of Christian community at work had it not been for one tiny detail: I had not once prayed a word for her father. Not only did I not pray; I had not even thought about him since our last discussion.

Know the feeling? Have you ever made a heartfelt commitment to pray for someone's need, and then completely misplaced the promise? How did you feel when someone thanked you for your prayers? What did you do or say at that moment?

If you are like me, you had feelings of guilt. On the phone, my friend was going on and on about how good she felt that I was praying for her dad. At that point I did pause and throw up a quick prayer so that I would not be a complete fraud, but I could not find the words to admit my failure. There was a lot more at stake here than confessing the shortcomings in my prayer life: this lapse in memory threatened to destroy the progress I had made with Lynn. I had been talking with her about faith for quite a while, and discussing her father's illness was the first serious spiritual conversation she had ever initiated.

I became determined never to let this happen again. Needless to say, after we hung up I was angry at myself. How could someone I cared for share such an urgent, personal, and important situation with me, and I completely forgot about it? Have you ever had someone update you on a prayer request you have completely forgotten about?

Part of the problem is that I can be terribly scatterbrained—maybe you can relate. There are so many details to manage every day, some are bound to get lost. I think that's true for most of us: we have so much going on in our own lives that we hardly have time to think about anything or anybody else.

How many times have these five words rolled off our tongues—*I will pray for you*—but without result? For me, more times than I want to recall, until I began prayer journaling. When I started using my Prayer Closet Organizer during my prayer time each evening, it caused me to think through my day and determine who needed—and who asked for—prayer. As those things come back to my mind, I write them down and take them to the Lord.

Pray Smart

When my girls were small, we had Sunday night devotions, and we always closed with prayer. We would circle around the table and share our prayer requests to record collectively in our family Prayer Closet Organizer. One February night, my daughter Kassie happily rattled off her prayer request for snow so she and her sister Kallie could stay home from school the next day.

This was a teachable moment. Ecclesiastes 5:2 says, "Don't be quick with your mouth or say anything hastily before God, because God is in heaven, but you are on earth. Therefore, let your words be few." I wanted my girls to be careful about what they brought before the Lord because their requests could have a negative impact on others. Praying for snow could be detrimental to drivers' road safety, jeopardize some people's jobs, not to mention increase the hardship some endure who do not have heat or the money to pay their heating bills. I reminded them to check the motives of their hearts before they form prayer requests. Our prayer petitions should be meaningful and for the good of God's will.

I have found it helpful to take a little time to consider exactly what it is I am praying for and why. Should I really pray that my cousin finds a new car? How do I pray through my friend's divorce? It is not always cut-and-dried.

For example, if someone has lost a job, maybe a new job isn't the right prayer. Scenarios of job loss can create a multitude of needs aside from the monetary ones. A person in such a situation may also need renewed self-confidence, stronger faith, wisdom about possible job contacts, and new opportunities—you can probably think of more. Over the years I have seen God take job loss and lead the unemployed person into ministry, into helping a loved one through a serious illness, and even into a completely different but more rewarding career. That is why every prayer request is special and unique, as well as complex and highly personal. For some, there is a lot at stake. In every situation, there are many facets to each need. Using your organizer can help you think through and record these varied needs and pray more effectively.

A Quandary: Healing

A couple of years after my husband and I were married, one of his dear aunts was diagnosed with stage-three lung cancer. I could not imagine Aunt Linda dying, and so I confidently announced to his family that I believed God would heal her. I sent her letters with Scriptures, took some of my friends to her home to have prayer with her, and clung to my faith in God's ability to heal her.

When she passed away, my first thought was to question why God had not taken this wonderful opportunity I had provided Him to demonstrate His miraculous healing power (a prideful viewpoint, I later realized). Second, I was mortified when I thought about seeing the whole family again; after all, I had been claiming Aunt Linda's healing for months. Would my unmet request confuse those who did not have a personal relationship with Jesus? Would the others doubt my faith in Christ? Would this give Christianity a black eye?

The family caravanned two hundred miles and up a mountain in Eastern Kentucky where the family cemetery was perched. There we laid Aunt Linda to rest. After the funeral I was pleasantly surprised when some of our family members thanked me for believing God for Aunt Linda's healing and shared how inspired they were through that experience.

Only God can take what may to us be disappointment and still be glorified in it. I do not understand why God chooses to heal some and not all, but I do understand He is love and He is sovereign. It is because of this truth that we can confidently pray for healing. Nowhere in Scripture are we discouraged from praying for a loved one's healing. In every instance where Jesus is petitioned for healing, He is agreeable. Never once does He scold someone or redirect a person to desire anything other than complete healing. Let this put your mind to rest when you are presented with a need for physical recovery—feel free to pray for healing against the gracious backdrop of God's sovereign will.

Ask, Seek, Knock

I confess, there have been times when I have looked at my weekly prayer worksheet and felt overwhelmed by the number and weight of my prayer petitions. When I came across a very familiar passage of Scripture a few years ago—"Ask and it will be given to you; seek and you will find; knock and the door will be opened to you" (Matthew 7:7 NIV)—it came to me that I could use this Scripture to further help sort my requests.

I began to write one of three letters beside each prayer petition. I placed an A beside those requests whose results are strictly out of my control. Some of these prayer requests are the most heart-wrenching. For instance, all I could do was "Ask" as a dear friend's son lay in a coma for months following a car accident. Other than try to comfort her, I could only ask God for a miracle. Some other examples of the appropriate times to "Ask" is when we pray for a loved one's safe travel, good test results from the doctor, and the safety of our military. We ask God for favor, rescue, help, and miracles in these situations. We can offer nothing but our prayer support.

We "Seek" when our prayer petitions *for ourselves* call for guidance and direction. Examples are prayers in regard to job changes, marriage partners, major purchases, and ministry endeavors. I place an S beside this type of entry, and then I begin to "Seek" God's direction in the matter. If I am expecting to hear a word from the Lord, I make sure, first and foremost, that I am reading God's Word daily. One thing I never do is just choose a Scripture and claim it for my situation. I have learned that if I am constantly in God's Word, His specific Word for my circumstance will find me.

Part of "Seeking" regarding my own personal needs may also include obtaining godly counsel. I have a small, intimate network of women whom I consider to be more spiritually mature than I am. I feel comfortable sharing my dilemmas with them because I trust their feedback. If I did not have an established group of mentors in my life, I would probably speak with my deacon's wife or another woman in my church whose godly wisdom I have witnessed. My husband is also a constant source of clarity. Prayer requests that require "Seeking" need more than just prayer; they require some effort on my part.

Related to the "Seeking" requests are those prayer petitions *for others* that demand movement, or "Knocking." Appropriately, I place a *K* beside the requests that require some specific action on my part. These efforts remind me I am partnering with God. Second Corinthians 6:1 tells us that we are co-laborers with the Lord in His kingdom work.

When we pray, God may give us a specific way to intercede for someone. Sometimes we are directed to be part of the solution or are led to provide an encouraging word at just the right time. This is how we work within the body of Christ. Prayer is not about giving a wish list to God and seeing how many requests get the answers we want. It is about our relationship with our Lord and being used on this earth in ways that glorify Jesus.

One of best examples of when to designate the *K* is when I am praying for someone's salvation. Just maybe God wants me to share my coming-to-faith story and the gospel message with that person. I used to pray over these kinds of requests in a very hands-off manner—leaving all the action strictly to God. It had become so easy for me to pitch up a petition and just leave it to Him. It finally dawned on me that maybe I should become God's coworker on this assignment. Why? It is not that God is not capable, but He has entrusted me, as well as other Christians, with the salvation message for one reason: to share it.

Action, or other forms of "Knocking," may be needed for reconciling friends, confronting an obstinate Christian with his or her sin, or correcting our very own bad habits. God's Spirit is at work in these scenarios, so why wouldn't I be, too?

The designation of Ask, Seek, and Knock gives me an effective prayer strategy. In light of this, why should I only ask that a relative come to know Christ, when I can be instrumental in sharing how he or she might do this? Does it make sense to ask only for wisdom but fail to read God's Word or seek godly counsel from a mentor? Only in issues that are completely beyond my personal influence should I simply ask God to intervene. Otherwise I should explore how His Spirit directs my actions to help bring about the answers I seek.

Use the Word to Give You Words

Another helpful prayer practice is to pray Scripture. Author and speaker Beth Moore writes, "I am utterly convinced that the two major weapons with divine power in our warfare are the Word of God and Spirit-empowered prayer."[1] Each section of the Prayer Closet Organizer has a correlating Scripture in the header. I typically pray that Scripture followed by my entries. Praying God's Word along with my prayer petitions sets my mind toward God's will. When I pray the Scriptures over my praise and worship, I am reminded of the absolute truths about God's goodness that I may otherwise overlook. When I pray the Scriptures over my Freedom and Forgiveness section, I am comforted by the magnitude of grace and mercy described in those short sets of words. In particular, when

I was recently feeling that a lot of things were falling through the cracks with my ministry work, I felt encouraged when I prayed, "Now finish the job as well so that you finish it with as much enthusiasm as you started" (2 Corinthians 8:11). It recharged me and readied me for service once again.

Organizing Your Prayer Closet

As you sit before the Lord today, review the following questions. Write the answers in your organizer.

- Were any prayer needs revealed to me today?
- Did I promise anyone prayer?
- What personal needs do I need to bring before the Lord?
- Which are Ask requests, Seek requests, and Knock requests?
- What actions do I need to take on behalf of myself? Of others?

When listing your prayer requests, make sure to be specific and don't forget to designate the A, S, or K. Here are some examples:

PRAYER PETITIONS
What are my
prayer requests?

*"Cry out to me whenever you are in trouble; I
will deliver you, then you will honor me."*
—Psalm 50:15

* Healing for Lynn's father (A)
* Direction for next step after my job loss (S)
* Reconciliation between Tina and Allison (K)

Based on these needs, I might pray the following:

Heavenly Father, Your Word says that we should cry out to You when we are in trouble, and that is what I am doing as I lift Lynn's father to You. Even though I don't understand how Your healing hand works, I want to acknowledge Your power. I call out to You for healing on his behalf, Lord. I ask that You touch his body.

Lord, You are aware of my job loss, and You know my future. Father, I need Your direction. I pray, God, that You will not only make provision for my family but also show me the next step during this time of uncertainty.

Last, God, I pray for my friends Tina and Allison. You know all of the issues behind their disagreement. Because You have called Your people to be peacemakers, I know that I should be a part of this much-needed reconciliation process. One thing I can do is to speak to them individually about Your forgiveness and the Scriptures You have given me that direct us to forgive one another. I trust in Your leading and Word as I proceed. Thank You for the opportunity to serve You in this circumstance.

> *He who has learned to pray has learned the greatest secret of a holy and happy life.*
> *—William Law[2]*

CHAPTER 5
GOD ANSWERS

I cry out to you because you answer me.
—Psalm 17:6

Up until the moment I began prayer journaling, I don't think I even realized that God answered my prayers. As I mentioned in the introduction, when I received a small, leather-bound prayer journal from one of my aunts for Christmas, it had two columns: Prayer Request and Prayer Answer. At first I was I excited by it, but then I became intimidated. I actually thought that my recordings in this new prayer journal might make God look bad. (Can you imagine?) Still, during the first week of recording my prayer petitions, I also recorded answers. After this exercise it became clear to me that God answered not only my prayers but also the prayers of others! A prayer journal does not make God "look bad"—quite the opposite.

As people who pray, though, we must face a certain fact: Although it is true that God answers prayer, it is not always with a Yes. Sometimes He says No or Wait. I can say that as I have used my organizer over the years, I have come to realize that God says Yes far more than He says No.

Sometimes, we need a clear picture of what God is doing in order to be encouraged in our prayer lives. This is where the Prayer Closet Organizer serves a life-giving purpose. At the end of the year, I tally up my prayer journal entries as part of a time of reflection. When I quantifiably look at what God has done, I continue to be amazed. Last year, I made 282 prayer petition entries in my organizer. I found that 189 were answered with a Yes, 27 received a No, and one request received a Wait response. I chose to carry over 47 "open" prayer requests into the new year. There were 18 prayer requests for which I did not know the outcomes; some were general in nature, like prayer for a bereaved family at church for whom I would pray until year's end. Here is an illustration of the year-end review I just described:

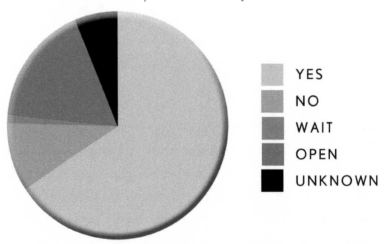

YES

NO

WAIT

OPEN

UNKNOWN

My prayer review clearly shows that my God is not a God of No. Do you realize this when it comes to your own prayer life? It just might be that until you have taken an assessment of what God is doing with your prayers, you are prone to think God says No more often than He actually does, beloved. I love the wording of Romans 8:35, 37: "Who will separate us from Christ's love? Will we be separated by trouble, or distress, or harassment, or famine, or nakedness, or danger, or sword? . . . But in all these things we win a sweeping victory through the one who loved us." Take another look at my illustration; I think it shows a sweeping victory in my prayer life!

The high number of Yeses in my chart may be an indication that my prayer petitions are more often in alignment with God's will than anything else. The consistent practice of bringing spiritual things into my physical view through prayer journaling has given me an uncommon advantage of better understanding God's direction. Years of evaluating God's responses to my prayers has helped me to craft, if you will, a higher quality prayer request. For instance, years ago, I may have inappropriately prayed that God would give a husband to one of my single girlfriends in hopes that she would settle down from her wild and promiscuous lifestyle. But a higher quality request is one that is more focused on eternal value. I may ask for opportunity to have a serious conversation with her about God. It could be, in fact, that God will use my girlfriend's singleness as a ministry in her life or a means of drawing her closer to God.

See how I have moved in my heart and my thinking regarding my friend's needs? The change offers a much more focused, productive, and valuable prayer request. This is one result from spending quality time in prayer: my desires become more aligned with God's, and this is much more valuable to me than getting what I might think is best.

God's Answers Are Sovereign

As much as I like to celebrate the Yes, it is just as important to accept the No answers. Receiving a No can be of as little consequence as when I pray for favor during a business meeting or as detrimental as not receiving healing from a terminal illness. While a Yes always makes me happy, my responses to a No can range from disappointment to devastation. I have heard it said that when God says No, He is really saying that He has something better planned, but that is a difficult thing to grasp when you have lost a loved one after prayer for his or her healing. It can be even more difficult to receive a No before you even had the chance to ask for something in prayer. But it is through these difficulties that we can learn more about God's love and mercy.

It was Black Friday all right, but not the typical kind where you spend the day Christmas shopping and end it with a sense of accomplishment and excitement for the upcoming holiday. It started out with shopping and cheer but ended in family tragedy. In a freak automobile accident, my brother-in-law Mike was taken from us and one of our nephews hospitalized with multiple injuries. Of all the ways death comes, it is the unforeseen senseless and tragic accidents that vex my soul the most. The shock and horror of these types of death are more apt to challenge my sense of God's love than any other. This was a case in which I received a No before I even had a chance to pray for Mike's survival.

In the days that followed, I dreaded the whole funeral experience. Seeing my nephews was heart-wrenching, and preparing for the services to come was almost too much to bear. I so did not want my nephews to have to endure this loss. I hated the thought of it all; their lives would be changed forever.

Despite its being November, the day of the burial was sunny. Mike was buried under a large, pretty tree. Just to the right of his plot was a statue of Jesus kneeling in the garden of Gethsemane. At first I found this a strange monument for a cemetery. I was more accustomed to the majestic concrete images of Jesus standing as if He has just returned to collect His bride, or a statue of a judgment seat—a daunting reminder that in the end we will meet Jesus face-to-face and give an account for our lives. The rendering of Jesus' prayer in the garden shifted my mind to its meaning during the graveside service.

As I thought about Jesus in this particular moment of His life, it was completely synonymous with my feelings over this whole experience. I did not want our family to endure such a horrific loss, and here was Jesus in the same situation. It was in the garden of Gethsemane where Jesus, too, stated His desire to avoid such immense pain, if at all possible.

> *[He said to the disciples,] "I'm very sad. It's as if I'm dying. Stay here and keep alert." Then he went a short distance farther and fell to the ground. He prayed that, if possible, he might be spared the time of suffering. He said, "Abba, Father, for you all things are possible. Take this cup of suffering away from me. However—not what I want but what you want." (Mark 14:34-36)*

What was most profound to me in this moment was that Jesus experienced what it was like to receive a No to His prayer request. There was no alternative to Christ's earthly experience, and there was now no alternative for my family.

Somehow this realization that God's only perfect and beloved Son had also received a No gave me comfort and strength. I could now more clearly see, with the help of this concrete visual aid, that Jesus does understand the grief we experience. He can identify with our pain and suffering. Not only did He witness it in others, such as when Mary grieved over her brother Lazarus's death, so much so that He too wept, but He also endured unbearable personal grief (John 11:33-35). And since Jesus personally bore such pain, He can comfort us in very real and understanding ways. In the days that followed Mike's death, I spent time processing what had happened and meditating on the Scriptures about Jesus in the garden of Gethsemane. It was through God's unfailing love that I found comfort during such a tragic time of loss. What are some ways that God has comforted you after a tragedy?

Who Is in Charge—Once and for All?

When we feel the pain of a No, we can begin to doubt God's existence and love for us. In my own personal season of pain and disappointment, I had to settle the matter of God's enduring love for me before I could move on. After my divorce, I was devastated by a painful event and a friend who knew I was not doing well called one afternoon to check on me. I remember her asking, "Gina, don't you believe in God's goodness and blessings?" I responded that I did; however, God must not have intended them for me. I was in this dark place where the pain overwhelmed my sense of God's unfailing love. If we wait to make the decision of God's existence, love, and goodness during a tragedy, our grief may default us to distrusting God. I needed to resolve to trust God no matter what, and had I made this decision long ago, I could have avoided a lot of self-inflicted pain. I either trust God's sovereign will or I do not.

What about you? Has a sudden loss caused you to wonder if God was real, if He loved you, if He could bring blessing out of any circumstance? Have you settled in your own mind that He is in charge—and that's a good thing?

A Scripture that has long impressed me is found within the devastating account of Job's losses. His words challenge me to respond even to God's most painful No with Job's very own words: "Though he slay me, yet will I hope in him" (Job 13:15 NIV). According to *Clarke's Commentary on the Bible*, Job is saying, "I have no dependence but God; I trust in him alone. Should he even destroy my life by this affliction, yet will I hope that when he has tried me, I shall come forth as gold."[1] This is my goal when I receive a No. I may not always react as well as Job did; the refining process is a slow and steady one, and I trust God will continually transform my will to His.

One of my settled beliefs is that the Lord God allows and disallows everything. With this mindset, I more easily accept God's sovereign will. Nothing comes to me that does not pass through God's hands (Job 1; Lamentations 3:37-38). That can be a disturbing truth if I am not resolved to commit my whole life to Jesus Christ. If I have determined that God is in control, and more than anything I want His will accomplished through me, I am comforted by the knowledge that He is watching every detail in my life.

Do I always understand God's will? Of course not. Twice I have been asked and agreed to speak at a local venue, but both times something has come up to keep me from my commitment. There is no reason to be upset over this; God has simply not allowed it. Maybe I acted presumptuously in accepting those speaking engagements in my eagerness to share the message God has given me. Maybe God was not willing to open that door to that particular audience just yet. My attitude that *God*—not fate or chance—allows and disallows everything keeps me from being overly upset and stressed. Can you think of a time where you felt sidetracked? Did you wonder if God was redirecting you or delaying your work for a different purpose in that situation?

Considering the Big Picture

Our human minds cannot fathom God's plans and how they are twined throughout our lives. But we do not have to understand all of God's plans to know His love for us is real and active. God's sovereign answers to my prayers continue to teach me more and more about my Lord. Through using my Prayer Closet Organizer, I have discovered the ability to ponder God's answers to my prayer petitions. I wonder why He has said No to some requests and what it means in relation to His extensive plans. There I find comfort that I cannot completely explain.

You see, in the warmth of God's in-control arms, I find refuge from events and circumstances I don't understand. I don't know why God heals one person, but not another. I wouldn't even pretend to know the heart and mind of God in many situations, but I do know that God loves all His children. God loves me and has a plan for my life. God loves you and has a plan for your life as well. God allows and disallows all that happens to us, and this can calm our minds. It can keep us from overreacting to life. If a door closes that I wanted to walk through, I accept that it is God's hand redirecting me. Sometimes the Lord is saying "Later" or "Take this other route." My responsibility is to discern God's direction and be steadfast in my faith, whatever comes.

My Lord's eyes see farther than mine, and God's ways and thoughts are greater than mine (Isaiah 55:8-9). Everything belongs to Jesus and is for His good pleasure and plans (Colossians 1:16). As we receive an answer from the Lord, may it be accepted against the backdrop of God's unfailing love and infinite wisdom.

Organizing Your Prayer Closet

It is important to record God's answers. I think you will be surprised to learn that God says Yes far more often than He says No in your life too. When God answers your prayers, please note the answer in this section of your Prayer Closet Organizer. You may also want to write a Y for Yes or an N for No so that you can quickly add them up at the end of the year. To ensure you include the most significant details when recording God's answers, you may want to:

- Describe the answer succinctly so it will be recalled with clarity.
- Describe how the answer came to be.
- Describe your feelings about your answer by utilizing punctuation or symbols, such as a smiley face.

Examples of how God has worked through my prayer petitions:

PRAYER PETITIONS

What are my
prayer requests?

*"What should I do? I'll pray in the Spirit, but
I'll pray with my mind too...."*
—1 Corinthians 14:15

* Asked to lead our Women's Ministry (S)
* Emma to have favor for purchasing a home so her
   children can join her from Nigeria
* Uncle Lou - Physical Healing
                        - Salvation

GOD ANSWERS

What is God's answer
to my prayer?

"Consider God's work!"
—Ecclesiastes 7:13

* Yes - God has given me a beautiful plan for women's
   ministry
* Yes - Emma just moved in!
* No - Uncle Lou passed away — 10/12
* No - Uncle Lou refused to see the visiting minister
   or even talk about salvation

During my prayer time, I use this department to acknowledge what God has done with my prayers. Based upon the entries above, I might pray something like this:

Sovereign God, just as Ecclesiastes 7:13 challenges me to consider Your works, so I have, and I stand in awe of Your wisdom, grace, and mercy shown in how You have answered each prayer petition. Because You have given me a beautiful women's ministry plan, I now know that I can confidently accept the position. Thank You for providing Emma with a home. I can't wait to meet her children who have longed to join her in the U.S. Despite the fact that Uncle Lou did not receive Christ as Savior before his passing, I am thankful that You provided him with plenty of opportunities to make that decision; You are merciful. I have considered Your works, I know that You are a loving and kind God. Even when I see the open requests, I am confident that You will answer me! I thank You for the Yeses and will not be discouraged by the Nos.

> *Four things let us ever keep in mind: God hears prayer, God heeds prayer, God answers prayer, and God delivers by prayer.*
> *—E. M. Bounds*[2]

CHAPTER 6
AT THE RIGHT TIME

*It is beautiful how God has done everything at the right time. He
has put a sense of eternity in people's minds. Yet, mortals still can't
grasp what God is doing from the beginning to the end of time.*
—Ecclesiastes 3:11 (God's Word)

My family will tell you that I am extremely time sensitive. They can't
stand it. Every evening I take my planner and schedule my next
day's activities so that I basically know what I will be doing at any given
hour. I plan the following day and most of the rest of the week. If you

think this an admirable quality, then try calling me up last-minute to interject yourself into my well-planned day! But without this obsession, I fear I would accomplish nothing.

As someone who likes to plan and keep records, I have found it especially helpful to write down the times God has moved in my prayer life in the Prayer Closet Organizer. It helps me see the wonder of His works:

> *Every thing is as God made it; not as it appears to us. We have the world so much in our hearts, are so taken up with thoughts and cares of worldly things, that we have neither time nor spirit to see God's hand in them. The world has not only gained possession of the heart, but has formed thoughts against the beauty of God's works.*[1]

When we record God's timing, we then can begin to see God's beauty.

Several years ago, after I was laid off during the economic downturn, I was immediately offered an unpaid position to lead our women's ministry. God had given me a wonderful vision for it; however, I could not see how I was going to be able to do it. My husband's immediate response to my layoff was for me to find another job.

I spoke with my pastor, explaining that I felt as if I were in a fog. I could not get a good feel for exactly where God was leading me. How was I going to commit to a full-fledged women's ministry on top of a new job? To this, my very direct but faithful mentor reminded me, "Gina, not everything that happens to you is about you!"

I wasn't offended by this because I understood his point. Fact is, the holding pattern I was in may have had more to do with my spouse, my children, or other people and plans than it had to do with me. And the question for me during this time was, could I wait for the Lord to work in those lives and plans despite my selfish need to know NOW how I could plan my life?

Sometime after this, when we arrived home from church, my husband unexpectedly said that he wanted me to take the year off and complete my bachelor's degree. I couldn't believe it, but I jumped at the idea of a one-year sabbatical, which would allow me time to kick off the new women's ministry. God had used the time delay to speak some things to my husband. Even though my husband's take on this sabbatical was from more of a practical standpoint than a spiritual one, God used it.

Eighteen months later, I went back to work at a job that a friend helped me obtain. Shortly after arriving, I realized that this particular company did not hire people without degrees. Had I not taken the time off in order to finalize my bachelor's degree, I would not have landed this job, friend or no friend. Within a year, that job disappeared, as there was a consolidation and restructuring, which ultimately took me to a part-time job allowing me to continue my women's ministry at church.

God paces the events of my life—and yours—as a well-timed dance.

In a world where mediocrity runs amok and poor customer service has become standard, one verse of Scripture reminds me about God's supremacy regarding timing. Second Peter 3:9 states, "The Lord isn't slow to keep his promise, as some think of slowness, but he is patient toward you, not wanting anyone to perish but all to change their hearts and lives." Everything He does is perfectly planned on His timetable.

In the Scripture I just shared, I notice God is conveying the message that timing is not so much about Him as it is more about us. God is waiting on me sometimes as much as I think I am waiting on Him. In our rushed lives, we are so put out by waiting in traffic, in doctor's offices, and in checkout lines. We have even become impatient with God when we are waiting on Him, as if His delays are a nuisance to us. Thanks be to God that He is willing to wait on us!

I Can Wait

I am keenly aware, and I'm sure you are, too, that God does not always work on a timetable that meets my needs. I still have some outstanding prayer requests to be answered. But because I have embraced Psalm 31:15, I can rest while I wait because I agree with David when he said to God, "My times are in your hands" (NIV). Whether I am waiting for a promotion, for healing, or for wisdom, my experiences are under the command and plan of Jesus Christ. I can wait because I know that God loves me and He will not leave me or forsake me (Deuteronomy 31:6).

The old adage "Timing is everything" is a common theme that showed itself to be true during Jesus' stay on earth. Although God is not bound by time, He does honor it by ensuring that His actions work perfectly within its confines.

> *When it was almost time for the Jewish Festival of Booths, Jesus' brothers said to him, "Leave Galilee. Go to Judea so that your disciples can see the amazing works that you do. Those who want to be known publicly don't do things secretly. Since you can do these things, show yourself to the world." His brothers said this because even they didn't believe in him.*
>
> *Jesus replied, "For you, anytime is fine. But my time hasn't come yet." (John 7:2-6)*

This Scripture perfectly describes my occasional attitude during prayer. No matter the prayer petition, my thought was, "Anytime now is fine for You to answer, God!" But God's timing is far too important to be casual about it. It has been said that Jesus came at the perfect time in history. The culmination of various prophecies to be fulfilled, the longing of Jewish hearts to be freed from Roman rule, and the infrastructure and civic upgrades of the Roman government all contributed to the perfect timing of Christ's birth, life, ministry, death, and resurrection. We may look at one situation in our lives without considering its impact on the larger picture. God is not so narrow-minded. This is why anytime is typically not the right time.

God knows how vital perfect timing is, so sometimes He asks us to wait for the answer we seek. Do you remember what we used to call servers in restaurants? We called them "waiters." A good waiter is a good server. A call to wait is as important as any calling in our lives. We should aspire to wait well. When we are called to wait, how can we best use that time to serve? Is there a particular scenario that you are currently waiting through? If so, how can you better serve God during this time?

Trusting Through the Waiting

Many years ago after being set free from a horrible situation, I felt God showed me a picture of my future. Afterward I felt as David did when God told him about everything He was going to do for David and his family (2 Samuel 7:11-29). All I wanted to do was sit in God's presence in complete awe and thankfulness. It was the epitome of Ephesians 3:20: "Glory to God, who is able to do far beyond all that we could ask or imagine by his power at work within us."

After several months of receiving multiple confirmations and seeing God orchestrate circumstances, I thought my vision was about to come to pass. God said it; I believed it; it was going to happen.

Then, just as I was approaching the "promised land," everything fell apart. The only word I could get from the Lord was Isaiah 40:31:

> *Those who hope in the LORD*
> *will renew their strength:*
> *they will fly up on wings like eagles;*
> *they will run and not be tired;*
> *they will walk and not be weary.*

59

He wanted me now to "wait," but my heart was not in it. I felt as if God had pulled the rug out from underneath me and that was a more painful thought than losing the dream. I allowed a seed of distrust in God to take root. Since I did not feel as if I could trust Him, I told the Lord that if I waited and He didn't come through, then I might forever walk away from Him.

I know now that I was in no position to make deals with God, but at the time my heart and my mind were so distressed that I felt this was my only recourse. I gave up on the wait and began to rebel against God for a season, and I stepped outside of what I knew to be God's intended will for my life.

For years, I wondered why God would show me a vision and then, just before bringing it to reality, say, "Wait." It was a great mystery. After about seven years of praying over it, I finally received the answer. Ready? I had not understood the wait! I thought the wait was in relation to one event, but it turns out the wait was hinged on a much later event. Had I waited I would have ended up in the middle of God's will. Since I had not, there were many years of doubting my calling and ministry because I knew I had been disobedient.

In His graciousness, God restored my life and ministry in such a sweet way with His loving-kindness. Even though God gave me a beautiful ending, I don't know if it can ever compare to what God had in store for me within His perfect will. Waiting on God makes a difference.

Give Me Patience—I Think

So often I hear women talking about their need for patience. There is a common saying that we should never pray for patience because God will increase the turmoil in our lives in order to teach it to us. Dear reader, may I say that is simply not true. If you are a Christian, you have the Holy Spirit living inside of you. And because you have the

Holy Spirit, you have the fruit of the Spirit: love, joy, peace, patience, gentleness, kindness, goodness, and self-control (see Galatians 5:22-23). As Christians, we are all endowed with the fruit of the Spirit, but we must employ it. A display of good fruit—the qualities of the Holy Spirit—identifies us as believers.

As you wait on God for His timing, ask yourself:

- Do I have a humble attitude based on the fact that God is perfect in His timing?
- Do I truly believe that God is in complete and sovereign control, and that He has a better view of the full situation than I do?
- Do I need to simply wait because I really don't understand all the wonderful things the wait is working out for my benefit on my behalf?

Your answers will help you use the Spirit-given patience you have through your faith in Jesus Christ.

Organizing Your Prayer Closet

God is always working in the appropriate space of time within His will. God is never too late, but He is rarely as early as we like. The Lord uses the gaps in time—the waiting—to build and test our faith, as well as to work out issues in others' lives. Our anxiousness is removed once we grasp this concept. When recording in your prayer organizer, be sure to write in the date God answered your prayer, whether it was a Yes, No, or Wait. Some weeks there will be few dates to write in for answered prayer; other weeks you may make several entries.

We should make note of when God answered our prayer petitions at exactly the right time. It makes for a good reminder of God's faithfulness and encourages us when the wait seems long. As you wait on God, here are some questions to use during your personal time of reflection; record the answers in your organizer.

- Recall a moment when God answered one of your prayers at exactly the right moment. Do you trust God to do the same in your current pressing matters?
- How have you consistently responded to God's timing? Have you been pleased with your response of faith or disappointed by your reaction of unfaithfulness to God? During this current season of waiting, how are you doing?
- When you think back over your prayer life, what have you learned about God's timing? How would that lesson apply during your wait?

When recording God's answers to my prayers, I log the dates of when it happened just like below:

> **PRAYER PETITIONS**
> What are my
> prayer requests?

*"For this reason, confess your sins to each
other and pray for each other so that you may
be healed. The prayer of the righteous person
is powerful in what it can achieve."*
—James 5:16

Clarity of mind and right answers for my exams
Betty's healing
Kallie - decision to take job at daycare during the summer

GOD ANSWERS
What is God's answer
to my prayer?

*"Answer me, L*ORD*, for your faithful love is
good! Turn to me in your great compassion!"*
—Psalm 69:16

> * *Yes. Passed all three!*
> * *Yes. Issue found and corrected by surgery*
> * *No. Her father was not keen on pay / gas cost*

AT THE RIGHT TIME
When did God
answer my prayer?

*"But me? I trust you, L*ORD*! I affirm, 'You
are my God.' My future is in your hands."*
—Psalm 31:14-15

> * *4/18 - I will graduate on time!*
> * *5/10 - She recovered in time to go on mission field
>   as planned*
> * *6/1 - Update: Better job - 3-day/wk & more pay*

Acknowledging the timeframe of when God answered my prayers sometimes gives me another glimpse into God's majesty. As such, I may pray something like this:

> *Father of all time, my times are truly in Your hands, and there is
> no better place for me, my prayer petitions, and the circumstances
> they represent. I may be able to move some mountains in my own*

strength to make things happen; but, God, over time I have resolved that I want only what You want and when You want it to come to pass. And until then, I will wait with patience and a servant's heart. I am thankful that I can graduate with my Bachelor's before returning to the workforce; it will look good on my resume! Thank You for resolving Betty's issue before her mission trip. Thank You for the Nos too. Kallie ended up with a much better summer job because she was willing to listen to her dad and wait. As usual, Your timing is perfect!

> *It is good for us to keep some*
> *account of our prayers, that we*
> *may not unsay them in our practice.*
> —Matthew Henry[2]

CHAPTER 7
MY HEART/MY PASSION

*We aren't trying to please people, but we are trying to please
God, who continues to examine our hearts.*
—1 Thessalonians 2:4

When I left my small hometown for college, I declared a major in
fashion merchandising. My decision to enter this field of study was
based upon a discussion with an upperclassman whom I greatly admired.
At a graduation party she said this would be her major, and in my desire to
be like her I decided it also would be mine. I had dated her ex-boyfriends,

so why not add this to the list, too? Kind of sad, isn't it? I don't know whether she followed through with that major, but I know I did not. Once I realized that sewing would be involved, it was a no-brainer for me!

Have you ever done that—tried to emulate someone you respected by copying his or her actions—only to find your feet didn't fit in those footsteps? The sad truth about declaring someone else's major was that it put me in jeopardy of declaring a life that was not my own, not part of God's will.

Thankfully, I came to realize that God had a ministry and message for me *as an individual.* He has specific plans and dreams for you, too.

A Path to Discovery

In the movie *Eat Pray Love*, Julia Roberts's character explains to her therapist that she has made time for everyone else but has not taken even two weeks of a breather to deal with herself between relationships. So begins her journey to self-discovery. I have been on a similar journey, not to discover myself but to find my God-given purpose for being on earth. Have you? Have you spent time thinking and praying about God's role for you in the world? This is what living is really all about.

I found I need a place to deal with myself—check my motives and spiritual progress—on a regular basis. This is the only section of the Prayer Closet Organizer that asks about me. In this section, I prayerfully try to gauge how I am fulfilling God's plans for me, how I am living out my hope-filled future. I capture my thoughts, my struggles, and my passions and pray over them regularly. I try to map out where God is leading me. Here I can disclose the most secret things of my heart.

I want laser-like ability to discern God's voice, but I also want the keen ability to translate His direction into a meaningful life purpose that I am passionate about. This is where we cross the threshold from being Christian consumers to becoming Christian contributors. Consumers are focused on experiencing great worship, hearing a good sermon, and anything else that feeds their spiritual stomachs. And while spiritual nourishment is important, we are responsible to take this spiritual bounty to make a contribution to this world. As contributors we have a divinely appointed impact on others' lives. Contributors' hearts and God-given passions display His glory. Just as a bird's song reminds us that it is doing what God designed it to do—glorify its Maker—so do our pure and holy passions bring praise to the One who made us.

Start with the Heart

It all begins with our hearts. During my high school years I struggled with understanding who I was, and what if anything made me significant. In the end, it was when my heart was completely dedicated to God that He began to reveal my significance to me.

The Friday night ritual was always the same: after a home game we assembled at a local fast-food restaurant, then caravanned out to Flat Bridge, a favorite meeting place. It was while sitting on the hood of a friend's car there that I had an overwhelming realization that God could see me—and the sin I was involved with. In that moment, the Holy Spirit was pricking my heart, and I knew the things I was doing, involving alcohol and promiscuous behavior, were not pleasing to God.

During my teen years I'd had little interaction with the things of God. When I was seventeen, God tried to get my attention that Friday night at Flat Bridge. I said to Him: "God, I will serve You when I get older. When I am married, with kids . . . maybe when I am about thirty years old and bored out of my mind, I will serve You. But right now I just want to enjoy my teenage life."

What a lie! I was not enjoying my teenage years; alcohol and sex were recurring problems. By the time I was twenty, I had come to the end of myself. I was so burned out after a summer of partying that I was not mentally prepared to return to college for my junior year. I decided that because I was still unsure about the fourth major I had declared, I would take the semester off.

I decided I would take my grandmother to church the next Sunday. I had been evaluating my life and had a sinking feeling that if I did not course-correct soon I might become a complete failure. My Nanny depended on others for rides, and I thought I might feel better if I did this kind act.

It had been seven years since I had been to the little church, but after being seated I knew that this was where I belonged. I had this overwhelming sense of mental, emotional, and spiritual cleanliness, such as I had not experienced since I was a child. I had been a prodigal, but I was now home.

Philippians 2:1-2 (NIV) says, "If you have any encouragement from being united with Christ, if any comfort from his love, if any common sharing in the Spirit, if any tenderness and compassion, then make my joy complete by being like-minded, having the same love, being one in spirit and of one mind." That day I knew profoundly that I was in desperate need of the encouragement fulfilled only by Christ, that I needed the comforting love of Jesus, and that I needed His tenderness and compassion in my sad little life. While sitting next to my Nanny, looking around at this old, familiar church, I knew I wanted my life to be about Jesus.

So, at the age of twenty, I became completely committed, heart and soul, to the Lord. Immediately, God did three things: He changed my vocabulary, He healed my depression, and He released me from the need for drugs and alcohol. I don't know why or how, but I was changed and renewed in that moment.

Eventually I married, settled down, went to work, had babies, and by the age of twenty-seven, I knew God was calling me to women's ministry. After a few years of trying to figure out how to develop this ministry, in frustration I asked God why He hadn't spoken to me when I was younger, so that I could have done things differently in order to live out this calling. He reminded me of that night I sat on the hood of a car at Flat Bridge and told Him that I would serve Him *later*. God waited patiently until I was in my thirties and serious about serving Him, just as I had requested.

One thing could have made a difference: the condition of my heart. Even though I was a Christian when I had the Flat Bridge discussion with God, my heart was not ready. Years later, when I finally wanted no one or no thing more than I wanted Him, my life's purpose began to spring up like a tulip on a spring day.

Before I could clarify my calling, my heart had to be dedicated to living for Jesus. The heart is a tricky thing—God said so in Jeremiah 17:9-10:

> *The most cunning heart—it's beyond help.*
> *Who can figure it out?*
> *I, the LORD, probe the heart and discern hidden motives,*
> *to give everyone what they deserve,*
> *the consequences of their deeds.*

Only when the Lord cleansed my heart and I turned back to Him could I begin to seek my calling.

Solving the Mystery

I have had many conversations with women who long to know what God has placed them on earth for. Our callings in life are perpetual. They are either ongoing or oncoming. We may be called to one thing only, or called to several successive ministries. The word *calling* may evoke a sense of fear or intimidation because we often associate this word with someone who has been called to preach the gospel or move overseas as a missionary.

When I was young I was convinced that God would make me do something I would absolutely hate, but I have found His calling in life to be the most beautiful experience I have ever known. He has captured my heart.

In 1994, I had a vision: I could see myself ministering to the women of my church in our fellowship hall. I believed this idea to be from God, because women's ministry was nowhere on my radar and I'd had little exposure to it; in those days few women ministered God's Word. I didn't rush out and schedule a class; I waited on the Lord.

In 1998, I was visiting another church. The women's Sunday school teacher showed a short video clip of a woman teaching God's Word—I had never seen anything like it. I felt God was clearly saying to me, "You are going to do this same thing." Confirmations followed, appearing when I least expected them, and I knew that God was calling me to ministry.

Years passed. I went through a divorce and changed churches. I had a couple of opportunities to minister, but nothing that looked like a real open door. I have probably hundreds of entries in this section of my Prayer Closet Organizer begging God for ministry opportunities.

Do you know the feeling? Have you been persistently seeking the Lord and asking Him for direction, clarity, purpose, passion? Be assured: He will answer.

Finally, after ten years, God opened "a great door for effective work" for me (1 Corinthians 16:9 NIV) when I was offered a women's class to teach on Wednesday nights and a women's Sunday school class. Since the day one of my pastors sat across a table in a meeting and said he believed I was called to women's ministry, God has continued to broaden my reach.

During my first class, it seemed as if the Holy Spirit reminded me of my original vision: There I was ministering to women of my church in the church fellowship hall just like my vision. The lesson? The journey to fulfilling our calling may be long, it may be winding, but it will bring you to God's destination. God is faithful.

Creative Callings

Every calling is not to a public ministry, but every calling will be something we are passionate about. It will impact people for the glory of God. One of my friends is called to foster children. Another visits orphans in Romania twice a year. One of the ladies at my church takes her dog to schools and nursing homes as a part of her ministry. Thank goodness God does not use a cookie-cutter approach when calling us into ministry. He is a creative God, so why wouldn't He be just as creative with our callings?

You have a calling, spiritual gifts, and special interests; when you are doing the things that cause you to employ each of these facets, you are in step with God. You then know you have a purpose, and that what you are doing has eternal value. God often prompts us to do things that take us out of our comfort zone; however, He always shows that we, with His power, are able to do whatever He says we can do. God makes our skills and desires fit beautifully with His plans for our lives.

If you are wondering what you are on earth for, you can start by learning what your spiritual gifts are. Books can help you with this, as can a pastor or mentor. Pay attention to the things you are good at: I'd received compliments and recognition for my speaking and leading. Since I did not recognize my calling while I was in college, I did not devote any of that educational opportunity toward ministry preparation, but in His graciousness God has used my secular job responsibilities to develop my skills. Take note of what God is teaching you through various avenues.

Finally, answer these questions: Is there a grand plan in your mind that excites you? Has God given you an idea of something that is good and noble to accomplish? If you say Yes to either of these questions, you may very well have a glimpse of your divine calling.

Organizing Your Prayer Closet

Here we begin to think beyond ourselves and more about what God is calling us to in kingdom work. When our hearts' desires line up with God's will, great things happen!

Contrary to popular belief, our lives are not all about us; they are about Jesus. Do we love God the way we should? Do we care what God's good pleasure is for our lives? Here is where we begin, with a daily assessment of our inner thoughts and discernments. Are we moving closer to the Lord? Closer to God's will? Here are some things to ask yourself; record the answers in your organizer:

- Has the Lord clarified any part of my calling today?
- What needs do I feel most passionate about?
- Have I received confirmation about something today?
- Do I have any personal fears or struggles that are hindering me? How can I resolve those?
- Has God opened a door for ministry? In what tasks do I find the greatest joy? Might these be my calling?

In this department, I note those things that are burdening my heart, and updates on my ministry and passions. Here are some sample entries:

MY HEART / MY PASSION
What is going
on with me?

*"God is the one who enables you both to want
and to actually live out his good purposes."*
—Philippians 2:13

** Excited that a new door of effective work has
been opened to me through blogging*

> *My heart is broken for abused and
> neglected children. How can you use me to help?
> *I pray for even more opportunities to utilize
> my spiritual gifts in kingdom work!

When praying over this department, I include my Scripture in the header in my prayer, and pray something like this:

> God, my Creator, You have overwhelmed me with Your divine schemes! Philippians 2:13 says that You are the One who enables us with a desire and ability to live out Your good purposes. May it not be wasted on me, Lord. Give me the wisdom and discernment to follow Your lead. I want to share Jesus with others, especially the abused and neglected little ones who are on my mind every night when I pray, and You know just the right way I should go about it. Show me, Lord! I desire to feel Your good pleasure in the things You have called me to do.

It is only when the whole heart is gripped with the passion of prayer that the life-giving fire descends, for none but the earnest man gets access to the ear of God.
—E. M. Bounds[1]

CHAPTER 8
AMBASSADOR NOTES

*I'm an ambassador in chains for the sake of the gospel. Pray so
that the Lord will give me the confidence to say what I have to say.*
—Ephesians 6:20

E verybody spends eternity somewhere" is a current emphasis at my
church. We have gone all-out to insure our church members keep this
thought in the forefront of their minds. Yard signs, T-shirts, and armbands
have been passed out by the hundreds. Why? Because no matter what
distracts us in life, this is a profound truth, so profound that it warrants

our continuous reminding. Since Eve ate the fruit of the forbidden tree, mankind's intimate relationship with God has been severed. Jesus came and died for us so that we may be reconciled to God. This was His mission, and it is our ministry and message.

In this section of the Prayer Closet Organizer you will want to record the names of persons you have ministered to today and include any specific details to aid you in your prayer time. This section is not only for listing the names of those you have encouraged in the name of Jesus; it may include ways you have used social media, ministered to others financially, and invited friends to church. This department of the Prayer Closet Organizer trains me to be mindful of witnessing on a regular basis—something I might otherwise neglect. It is so easy to get caught up in the running, doing, and playing of life. But as I review this section daily, I am reminded that if I accomplish nothing else, I must be committed to sharing Jesus.

When I am witnessing to someone, one thing I try hard to do is actually say the name "Jesus" to qualify it as a witness. I am not sharing just any god with people; I am talking about the God who sent His Son, Jesus, to die on a cross for us. The name of Jesus carries power and influence; it is sacred to share with others, the name of the King of the universe. Everybody spends eternity somewhere, and *Jesus* is the eternal name by which eternal life comes!

In God's Eyes

Each of us has our own circle of influence. Daily we come in contact with people in need of encouragement, counsel, love, grace, and mercy. We are given varying opportunities to be Christ's ambassadors, and this is the place in prayer where we stop for a minute to recall those moments. My moments may include sharing an encouraging word with a coworker; maybe I prayed with a friend. Sometimes sharing the Lord is more about our actions than words. There is a passage in God's Word that is like a little spiritual handbook to me. Second Corinthians 5:16–6:10 states that I am an ambassador of Christ, and it also instructs how I am to go about being an ambassador.

The first thing I glean from this Scripture is that I serve an equal-opportunity God: "From this point on we won't recognize people by human standards. Even though we used to know Christ by human standards, that isn't how we know him now. So then, if anyone is in Christ, that person is part of the new creation. The old things have gone away, and look, new things have arrived!" (2 Corinthians 5:16-17).

My human perspective is distorted by my preferences and prejudices. I must remember that there was a period of time when people looked at Jesus from a worldly view; they didn't comprehend who He was: God in the flesh. To many He was simply a carpenter's son, an average kid from Nazareth, the boy next door. In human eyes He was too "normal" to be God. In God's eyes He was His beloved Son. We need to use God's eyes when we look at other people.

On the flip side, we sometimes think too highly of others and consider them unreachable.

My friend Tracey is one of the most beautiful women I have ever known. I first met her when I went to work for her uncle's business many years ago. She was so striking it was hard to stop staring at her. She was a very tall, very attractive, and very intelligent woman. She carried herself with such poise that she exuded class. Her regal looks, confidence, and communication style made her seem like a celebrity.

One day God prompted me to share Jesus with her. My initial thought was, *Are You kidding?* I could not imagine that I would have anything to share that would be of any interest to her. She did not know me or anything about my relationship with God. I did not understand how I could help her see she had a need for Jesus when it appeared as though she had everything.

I admit it: I felt inferior to her.

I prayed about what to do. Since I could not work up the nerve to witness to Tracey, I did the next best thing: I invited her mom, who worked with us, to come to church. Joanne and I had developed a good rapport and she gladly accepted my invitation. And guess who she brought with her?

To make a long story short, both of these beautiful, smart women fell head over heels in love with Jesus. Today, Tracey is one of my favorite Christian speakers. Nobody is too good to be introduced to Jesus. Nobody is without a real need for Jesus.

Despite all of our differences in race, creed, color, religion, gender, national origin, ancestry, age, marital status, or disability we can all come to receive Jesus Christ as Savior and be forever changed. Have you ever known someone who had a checkered past, then came to know Christ, and you had a hard time overlooking that person's history? So much so that it was hard for you to accept him or her as part of the family of believers? Maybe you know someone like Tracey, who seems to have all the best worldly attributes, who seems intimidating. Whether the people we encounter are Christians or not, we must not regard them with a worldly perspective. No one is off-limits to the salvation message. There is not one created human being whom God does not want to save. Not one person has sinned so greatly that he or she cannot be redeemed by the work on the cross. As such, allow this section of the organizer to be your constant reminder to demonstrate the grace and mercy of God on Jesus' behalf.

Many Ministries, One Goal

The next section in our handbook gives our objective for being one of Christ's ambassadors. Paul wrote, "All of these new things are from God, who reconciled us to himself through Christ and who gave us the ministry of reconciliation" (2 Corinthians 5:18). As Christians, we each have our own individual ministries but the same goal: reconciling others to God. Jesus Christ is the great Reconciler. It is our privilege to introduce sinners to the Savior. This is why we are not immediately ushered into God's presence once we receive Jesus as Lord: we have been given the ministry of reconciliation.

According to our handbook, our mission field is the world. Second Corinthians 5:19 says, "God was reconciling the world to himself through Christ, by not counting people's sins against them. He has trusted us with this message of reconciliation." God has left us a trust where we as Christians have custody of the lost. We are to take responsibility for those God has placed in our lives, insuring they are introduced to Jesus.

My ministry handbook not only gives me a job title, but a job description, and it is found in 2 Corinthians 5:20: "We are ambassadors who represent Christ. God is negotiating with you through us. We beg you as Christ's representatives, 'Be reconciled to God!'" How do we negotiate? How do we go about ministering the message of reconciliation? *Barnes' Notes on the Bible* states that we "are sent to make known the will of the sovereign, and to negotiate matters of commerce, of war, or of peace, and in general everything affecting the interests of the sovereign among the people to whom they are sent."[1] The span and scope of our job description as ambassadors for Christ provides us the ample opportunity to represent Jesus through the various positions we hold. This is why some Christians are involved in business, government, education, and many other areas where God has divinely placed them. In what areas are you experiencing success regarding the ministry and message of reconciliation? Do you need to be more intentional in your assigned areas of influence as Christ's ambassador? If so, how so?

What a Boss!

According to my handbook, I have a great employer! People in our position report to God. "We work together with him," Paul wrote in

2 Corinthians 6:1. One of the most important components of job satisfaction is based upon our perception of and relationship with the person to whom we report. There can be no better boss than God. We can trust that every decision made is right for every person involved. Because God made the personal sacrifice of Jesus, we know that we will never be asked to do something God would not be willing to do as well. Our God was a progressive leader—a hands-on, team-building kind of leader—before trendy terms like *servant leadership* or *transformational leadership* were in vogue.

Dealing with people can be messy. If they were perfect, they wouldn't need Jesus! I need to remind myself that my job responsibility is to implore people to be reconciled to God, and that sometimes means I must get down in the ditches with them to help them out. Whom do you need to serve? Do you know someone who needs help from his or her mess? Remember, we are not just working for God, but *with* God. What a privilege!

When Should We Show Up?

Our work hours have been defined in 2 Corinthians 6:2: "He says, *I listened to you at the right time, and I helped you on the day of salvation.* Look, now is the right time! Look, now is the day of salvation!" Our work hours as ambassadors for Christ are *now*. Never will you have such work hours in any endeavor that you dare to undertake. Paul challenged us: "Take advantage of every opportunity because these are evil times" (Ephesians 5:16). When I meet a person who needs help, I think about how I can respond in a way that points the person to Jesus while meeting his or her needs. Recently, I was helping someone prepare for a job search. It opened the door to discuss ways that God can lead us to something as practical as our next job and that, because He has called everyone into ministry, He will often place us where we can be used and developed for that calling. It is conversations like these that I record in the Ambassador Notes section.

We are spiritual beings who must be on our spiritual toes, making spiritual assessments of every situation that presents itself to us. As we interact with others, we should be mindful of the Holy Spirit's leading. With so much at stake, how can we ever be off-hours?

A Standard of Behavior

No handbook would be complete without rules of conduct. Second Corinthians 6:3-10 lists them:

> *We don't give anyone any reason to be offended about anything so that our ministry won't be criticized. Instead, we commend ourselves as ministers of God in every way. We did this with our great endurance through problems, disasters, and stressful situations. We went through beatings, imprisonments, and riots. We experienced hard work, sleepless nights, and hunger. We displayed purity, knowledge, patience, and generosity. We served with the Holy Spirit, genuine love, telling the truth, and God's power. We carried the weapons of righteousness in our right hand and our left hand. We were treated with honor and dishonor and with verbal abuse and good evaluation. We were seen as both fake and real, as unknown and well known, as dying—and look, we are alive! We were seen as punished but not killed, as going through pain but always happy, as poor but making many rich, and as having nothing but owning everything.*

Our behavior has a direct impact on our effectiveness in our reconciliation ministry. As the Scripture states, we will have our good moments in which our witness for Christ will thrive, and moments when we will be challenged to represent Him well. The first point Paul makes in this passage is that he does not want his behavior ever to keep anyone from meeting Jesus. How do we treat our spouses? How do we respond when we become upset in a public setting? How do we handle conflict and hurt feelings with others? These are just some of the things we need to pay attention to. What behaviors do you habitually exhibit that might be a hindrance to sharing the gospel message? It is important that God's kingdom is made up of a people who are committed to excellence and integrity. As ambassadors we are ministers. If you have never thought of yourself as a minister, start now. We are all in this together! Our witness, in word and action, matters because everybody spends eternity somewhere!

Organizing Your Prayer Closet

There are so many people in our lives: loved ones, friends, acquaintances, coworkers. Not one is there by accident. It is our privilege, as Christ's ambassadors, to share His gospel with them and to act with integrity in our lives. Throughout our day, we have so many opportunities to introduce Jesus to others. Sometimes we invite people into conversation about higher things by sharing our experiences, hopes, and dreams. We encourage people with Scripture, prayer, and our coming-to-Jesus testimonies. We minister to people financially, emotionally, and practically. The mention of the name *Jesus* is powerful, even in passing. If we think about our ambassador status daily, it will become a job description that we will be more intentional about in our transactions with others. Here are some things we can take note of in our Prayer Closet Organizers:

- Did I encourage anyone today?
- Did I share Jesus with anyone today?
- Did I invite anyone to church or a special church event?
- Did I identify myself as a Christian to anyone today?
- Did I publicly minister to anyone by speaking up or using social media?

- Did I demonstrate my Christianity in any particular situation today?

In this section, I log any instances where I ministered Jesus in some form or fashion to another. Some of my examples have included:

> **AMBASSADOR NOTES**
> Who did I share
> Jesus with today?

> *"The Lord has anointed me. He has sent me
> to preach good news to the poor, to proclaim
> release to the prisoners and recovery of sight to
> the blind, to liberate the oppressed."*
> —Luke 4:18

* Invited our new neighbors to visit our church
* Provided scholarship money for a needy child
  to attend church camp
* Loaned Liz my book about overcoming depression
* Updated my coworkers on God's
  healing intervention for my uncle

While praying through my Prayer Closet Organizer, I include the header's Scripture along with entries as follows:

Savior, thank You for anointing me to share the good news of Jesus with those around me. I pray our new neighbors will visit church this Sunday; it wasn't just an invite to visit our building, but an invitation to meet You. God, You richly bless the needy child that benefits from the scholarship money. I pray his or her life will be changed forever! Lord, as Liz reads the book, I pray that You will use the godly precepts contained within to free her from the bondage of depression. I pray my coworkers were impressed with Your healing grace for my uncle and will call upon You in their own time of need. You are a sufficient God!

> Prayer is the way you defeat the devil,
> reach the lost, restore a backslider,
> strengthen the saints, send missionaries out,
> cure the sick, accomplish the impossible,
> and know the will of God.
> —David Jeremiah[2]

CHAPTER 9
INSIGHT AND UPDATES

God revealed his hidden design to us,
which is according to his goodwill and the
plan that he intended to accomplish through his Son.
—Ephesians 1:9

Why do people seek out psychics, mediums, and tarot card readers? I would venture to say it is because they are looking for special insight. They want to know where their lives are headed, who might be in their future, or what they will be doing five years from now.

Perhaps these are some of the reasons Saul, the king of Israel, inquired of a medium in 1 Samuel 28. Israel's prophet and Saul's mentor, Samuel, had died and Saul was facing a war. Fearful and desperate to find out how it would end, he visited a medium to channel Samuel for insight. This was Saul's downfall: a constant disregard for God's instruction. When we as believers want more spiritual insight, we need to turn to God and His Word.

Living lives in which we are led by God is so much more meaningful and rewarding than trusting the words of diviners and mediums, whose sentiments mean nothing more than the scribbling inside a fortune cookie. God wants us to come to Him for wisdom and insight, and we go based upon one thing: our trust in God. He may not give us every detail we are looking for; this is partly because He wants us to live lives of real faith and partly because God longs for His children to come to Him, seeking wisdom. The more we study and understand God's Word, the more we can apply its truth to our individual situations and live in confidence.

We may know how our story ends ultimately, but sometimes the other details of our lives can, without our trust in God, lead us down a path of worry. Scripture gives us many promises to lean upon when we face the unknown.

Trust Takes Time

Have you ever done something extreme in order to get some "inside" information? Have you gone too far with an inquiry because you just had to know something? What do you do when you feel starved for details?

For the most part, we prefer to be aware of what's happening. If layoffs are coming at work, we want to know now if we will be affected. We want to see what is under the wrapping paper under the Christmas tree. When a new romance begins to flourish, we are frantic to know the feelings of the other person.

Typically we can find ways to get the scoop. We can unwrap and rewrap gifts without anyone's knowing. We can get information from the friends of the person we are dating. But with God, not so much. We must employ the fruit of patience in waiting for Him to divulge any special insight, and we cannot learn anything without spending valuable time with Him.

Periodically I go back through my organizer entries and evaluate the progress in the situations I have recorded there. I am frequently amazed at how the circumstances are developing under God's sovereign hand. This approach, recording prayer requests and following up on their development, is far superior to any other method I can come up with to ascertain how a matter will end.

It's funny that while we do not mind making sometimes shady deals to obtain information, we are so much less committed to resting at Jesus' feet to obtain spiritual insight. Sometimes we'd rather ask others for their advice or even seek the devil himself (disguised as someone less dangerous) than spend time with our Lord and Creator.

But God's insight can give us peace amidst the direst circumstances. When I can add an update to a prayer petition or realize I have been armed with some additional insight, I recognize that I am not alone in this world. What insight or updates have you received from God?

Trust Changes Eyesight—and Insight

In 2 Kings 6, the nation of Israel was encompassed by an enemy country, Aram. God's prophet, Elisha, showed uncommon confidence even as the Arameans surrounded his people. We can understand the anxiety of Elisha's servant when he "saw an army with horses and chariots surrounding the city. [He] said to Elisha, 'Oh, no! Master, what will we do?'" (v. 15). To him, there seemed to be no way out.

Elisha viewed the situation differently: "'Don't be afraid,' Elisha said, 'because there are more of us than there are of them'" (v. 16). Elisha knew all about resources of which his mystified servant was ignorant. "So the prophet prays that the servant's eyes may be opened, until with his inner vision he could see the vast host of unseen allies."[1] Scripture records, "Then the LORD opened the servant's eyes, and he saw that the mountain was full of horses and fiery chariots surrounding Elisha" (v. 17). In times when I feel overwhelmed by the enemy, I am able to review the Insight and Updates department and be reminded that Psalm 34:7 states that I am surrounded by God's protecting angel. This protects my mind and faith.

It is through prayer journaling that we tap into those unseen resources that can provide spiritual insight, peace, and confidence. This department of the Prayer Closet Organizer opens eyes and bestows insight. What godly insight or updates do you see in any of the situations for which you are praying?

A Glimpse of God's Hand

When we write down our prayer petitions, we truly surrender our worries, our confusion, and our need to know how things will turn out. Our strokes of the pen symbolize the release of our petitions into God's hands. It was fear of the unknown that drove Saul to consort with the wicked. It is to faith in God's providence and provision that we surrender.

In the King James Version, faith is defined in Hebrews 11:1 as "the substance of things hoped for, the evidence of things not seen." In the Insight and Updates section of my organizer I write in the evidence of my faith regarding my prayer petitions and other things of a spiritual nature. Over time as I pray, I can begin to see God moving in each situation, and although the answer has not yet come, I can catch a glimpse of God's hand.

First Kings 18 wonderfully displays this very scenario. After a showdown with evil prophets on Mount Carmel before King Ahab, wherein God's prophet Elijah performed miracles that displayed God's power, Elijah announced the first rain to come in several years: "Get up! Celebrate with food and drink because I hear the sound of a rainstorm coming" (1 Kings 18:41). To await the storm, he then climbed the mountain and there, bowed down.

Over and over Elijah sent his assistant, Obadiah, to go see if rain was indeed coming. Finally on the seventh trip Obadiah saw a small cloud. From that report, Elijah told King Ahab to "go down the mountain, and don't let the rain hold you back." What then? "A wind came up with a huge rainstorm" (vv. 44-45).

We can use our Prayer Closet Organizer much as Elijah used his servant. As we record our various prayer requests, the Insight and Updates section will help us check to see God at work in our situation. We may go back multiple times before we recognize God's hand. But when we do so, we can rest in that same confidence Elijah did for the rain. Sometimes the slightest development in our situation is enough to stoke the fire of our perseverance and conviction that God is in control. Do you see any new developments with your current prayer requests? If so, how will this help you persevere?

Step by Step

Through my prayer organizer I have found that God likes to show me what the end will look like, and then piecemeal me the rest. Does He do this with you, too? Sometimes I know where I am supposed to end up, whether it is in a simple matter or in something weightier like ministry efforts, but I have to wait until God gives me my next step to get there. This has been His method of operation for others as well, including the Old Testament hero Joseph. Joseph received a marvelous vision for his future. Though he was not sure how it would come to be, he did know that someday he would be in a position of authority. After his vision, events took him from being a favored son to being a target for murder, a slave, and then a prisoner before he was able to assume his long-awaited high position in Egypt (see Genesis 37–50).

How about you? Have you ever sensed God telling you how a situation would turn out, only to face a long wait and many challenges? Did you ask God continuously to confirm His promise? How did you maintain your faith?

In Joseph's case, God allowed the vision to come to the brink of death before He fulfilled it. In some instances, we may have this same experience. Our journey to God's destination is not always the scenic route; sometimes it is a trial by fire that purifies our hearts and motives while we're on our way to receiving the promise.

When we pray for ourselves and others we may see ups and downs, twists and turns, but may they be used as spiritual markers to guide us in prayer. Clarity for effectual prayer comes by taking note of spiritual insight and updates. By using our Prayer Closet Organizer to record our journey of prayer, updating it step by step, we can gain knowledge about how God brings His promises to us.

Unlocking the Secrets

Spiritual insight is as beneficial to intercessory prayer as a medical history is to a primary physician. It unlocks the secrets behind our individual situations. All people have a story, and their prayer needs are often tied to their life histories. We cannot know everything about someone for whom we are praying, but as Deuteronomy 29:29 states, "The secret things belong to the LORD our God. The revealed things belong to us." And so we take what is revealed to us and make good use of it in our prayers. When engaging in prayer, we may discover intercessory needs in various ways.

The old adage "Actions speak louder than words" tells us a person's behavior and also gives us clues that can show us how to pray for them.

I have a girlfriend, Jennifer, who is somewhat of an extreme gift giver. She is constantly and eagerly giving gifts to her friends, coworkers, and neighbors. There were times when the gifts were inappropriate based upon the relationship. She had always done this, but when she became an adult, the gift giving became more extravagant. Over time, many of our mutual friends stopped inviting her to join us because of this very issue; the gifts made them feel uncomfortable.

My initial thought was to pray that our friends would overlook her oddities, but after a few days I felt that was not the correct prayer request. I recalled a discussion I once had with her where she disclosed the reasons she gives gifts: it was to gain love and acceptance. Therefore I changed my prayer to a request that she would be healed from the neglect she had experienced during her childhood and find the acceptance and grace of God, which would provide her with the love she had been looking for.

Receiving spiritual insight and making updates to our prayers is one of the most effective tools we can use. For me, it takes what may look like a one-dimensional, flatly written journal entry and turns it into a three-dimensional issue. Whether I gain more spiritual understanding or the excitement of seeing God's hand on my prayer petition, Insight and Updates better engages me for more effectual prayer.

Organizing Your Prayer Closet

The Lord orchestrates our lives like a grand symphony, bringing all the notes together as sweet music. God is in control; I am confident. Our prayer requests are not always quickly answered, but that does not mean we cannot see the evidence of faith. It is an encouragement to capture God moving in a situation. Keep your eyes peeled for ways God may be acting in the situations and people you pray about. When you see a change, update your organizer. You're creating a record of God's faithfulness.

Here are some things to ponder; record the answers in your organizer:

- Has anything happened today that demonstrates God at work in any matter that I am praying for?
- Is there anything to update regarding previous prayer requests?
- Has God impressed upon me to pray in a very specific or urgent manner over any matter?
- Do I feel as if God has given me better spiritual understanding of a matter?
-

In this section, list your prayer request updates along with any special insight God has given you regarding your petitions. Here are some sample entries:

INSIGHT & UPDATES
What am I seeing God
do with my prayer?

"The one who searches hearts knows how the Spirit thinks, because he pleads for the saints, consistent with God's will."
—Romans 8:27

* Update: Bob & Lucy have decided to go to counseling
* Insight: Bob's mom's negativity toward Lucy may be the problem.
* Update: Cindy has a new job with great Christian coworkers

Here is a sample prayer for this section. It includes my Scripture from the header and my entries.

Lord, Your Word says in Romans 8:27 that You "search hearts," and I am glad that You do. While I am thankful that Lucy and Bob have decided to go to counseling, I pray that their hearts will be open and receptive as well as dedicated to their assignments. Lord, please direct them to a godly therapist. Lord, I may have caught some special insight into their situation today when Bob's mother was talking to me about Lucy. If this is the case, I pray for her to be a supporter of their marriage instead of an instigator. Father, I am very excited about Cindy's new relationship with her Christian coworkers. I have been a witness to Cindy for years, and now You have introduced some reinforcements to her daily life. I pray that their witness will make an impact. Thank You for sharing the evidence of my faith today in these prayer petitions. I am encouraged!

We must begin to believe that God, in the mystery of prayer, has entrusted us with a force that can move the Heavenly world, and can bring its power down to earth.
—Andrew Murray[2]

CHAPTER 10
EARS TO HEAR

Let the person who has ears, hear.

—*Matthew 11:15*

O ne of the greatest things I have discovered about God is that He likes to talk. He likes to talk and tell people about His upcoming plans. God told Noah He was going to send a flood. God told Moses He was about to rescue the Hebrew slaves. God told David he would be the next king of Israel.

God is selective about whom He shares His plans with; He tells only those who need to know—those who will be a part of the specific plan He is sharing. This is very exciting, provided that we are able to hear God's voice for ourselves. From what I gather, God flat-out told Noah about the Flood, He spoke to Moses from a burning bush, and He sent a prophet to anoint David as king. God speaks in a multitude of ways, and what an accomplishment it is to learn to hear Him.

The purpose of this section of the Prayer Closet Organizer is to capture those moments when God speaks to us—and He absolutely does. God may communicate with us about a job change, lead us to join a particular ministry, or prompt us to do something as simple as prepare a home-cooked meal for our sick neighbor. Because God has important things to share, it is crucial that we are able to hear Him.

Be Faithful to Read and Pray

I have not always been able to discern God's voice. For many years one Scripture bothered me every time I came across it: "Whenever he has gathered all of his sheep, he goes before them and they follow him, because they know his voice" (John 10:4). I knew this Scripture was basically saying that if I am a Christian, I will know the Lord's voice. The problem was that then, I really did not know when God was speaking to me about anything. I was not able to live this Scripture.

Over time, I have discovered that reading and knowing God's Word take much of the guesswork out of discerning what God wants me to do. For instance, God has laid out specific reasons for divorce, so we would know that if our scenario does not fit within His guidelines, divorce is not His will for us. By God's written Word, I believe that I should give 10 percent of my earnings to my church; I am not left to come up with my own tithing formula (Malachi 3:10; Hebrews 7:1-28). Furthermore, if I come across someone who is in need, I know I should help him or her.

But what about that guidance you need from God that is not specifically outlined in the Bible? I have found that whether I am reading the Bible or other resources such as my Sunday school lesson, a devotional, or Scriptures in my Prayer Closet Organizer, God will use His Word to speak to me. When we are continuously feeding upon God's words, His specific direction for our circumstance will find us. That is when we know we have a promise from God about a particular circumstance. Nothing can take the place of a healthy diet filled with the spiritual milk of God's Word, which is why Peter wrote, "Like newborn babies, crave pure spiritual milk, so that by it you may grow up in your salvation" (1 Peter 2:2 NIV).

Likewise, if I spend consistent time in prayer, I will develop an ear that becomes familiar with the ways God speaks to me. If I am not having consistent conversations with God and trying to follow His lead, then I cannot expect to ask a question of Him and have the ability to recognize His answer. It takes time to build a comfort level for recognizing God's voice. Nothing can take the place of experiences that mature us in the Lord, most of which are a result of a healthy prayer and devotional life.

Years ago, a company I worked for announced its plans to close the manufacturing facility where I was the human resources manager. The project team sent to shut down the facility treated our management group as if we were invisible. Being in the middle of this depressing situation at work weighed heavily on my mind. But during one of my pity parties, I decided that regardless of what was going on, I needed to continue doing the best job I could. After all, I was still employed and drawing a paycheck.

In my Prayer Closet Organizer, I noted three things I felt I should do: First, I had to get over the fact that I was no longer a decision maker at work. Second, because other people were now in charge, I needed to let go of my pride. Third, I knew that I should be helpful to the project team because it was the right thing to do.

Later that week, as I was reading some Scripture, I came across Proverbs 16:3, which says, "Commit your work to the Lord, / and your plans will succeed." At that moment, I felt God was highlighting these words for me and reminding me of my three decisions—which had now become my three directives from the Lord.

Months passed and I continued to follow these guidelines, and I began preparing my mind for a job search. One day, while praying the Scripture headers of my Prayer Closet Organizer, the verse for the "Ears to Hear" section stood out to me, and I immediately felt God speaking to me about keeping my job: "Stand firm. Let nothing move you" (1 Corinthians 15:58 NIV). I responded to God, saying, "Lord, I am not leaving my job—my job is leaving me!" Yet the Scripture came with clarity and I decided to act on those words.

A few days later, when the regional manager was visiting my facility, I told him that I wanted to stay on and asked about doing project work for our corporate office. Within a couple of weeks, I was reassigned to a corporate position, which prolonged my job for a couple more years.

Because I committed myself to God's three directives (committed my work to the Lord), my request for a special projects assignment was approved (my plans succeeded)—just as Proverbs 16:3 declared.

Surround Yourself with Wise People

Mentors are wonderful resources when we have questions. These are folks whose faith is more mature than ours. You should not be afraid to choose mentors who think differently from you. My first mentor was my Aunt Clarise, who was always concerned about my Christian growth. She never hesitated to challenge my thinking. Author Don Matzat writes, "Be willing to speak to individuals who may correct you, disagree with you, or warn you . . . but who also love you."[1] When godly people disagree with you, you should pause and reassess the direction you believe God may be leading you.

As a young adult, I met a fireball of faith named Joyce. This petite woman often spoke with power and might at the end of the service in my small, country church; it was almost like hearing a second round of preaching. She led many successful outreach efforts in our little church. Early on, I recognized that everything Joyce set out to do, she accomplished, and that was because she was able to discern what God was leading her to do. I wanted to know what she knew. It was this proven track record of faith that drew me to her as a student of how God could impart His plans for execution to His saints.

What special people might serve as godly examples to you? Who stands out as someone with special insight, a generous heart, and an approachable demeanor? Think of a few folks who might be willing to share their experiences of following God in new directions when you're in need of wise counsel, and seek them out. Godly men and women are a wealth of spiritual knowledge, and we all need someone we can take our questions to. When you can't tell what God wants you to do, a good leader can probably help you sort it out.

Keep a Record of Times You Seek God's Guidance

The more time I spend praying and journaling in my Prayer Closet Organizer, the more I learn to know God's voice. When I document how the Lord leads me in a given situation, I can look back later and see how I came to recognize His direction. As I go back and read all the entries that I made the year God was telling me to keep my job, it is the clearest demonstration I have as proof that God does lead His sheep with spiritual milk, with His Word, and by prayer. Whether we are fretting over our jobs, seeking guidance for parenting, or facing a difficult decision, if we have ears that hear, God will guide us.

Proverbs 20:24 says that our steps are ordered by the Lord. God had ordered my steps so I could keep my job. Had I reacted poorly at work to those who were now in authority over me and mistreated my project team, I would not have been recommended for a corporate position. When I look back, I know God was working on my behalf, and it is a life event I refer to again and again as a point of reference for hearing God when I am prayer journaling over other matters.

Keeping a record of my prayers and God's answers grows my faith. And it helps me learn to know my Shepherd's voice.

When God Speaks About Someone in Need

I have also experienced times when the Lord gave me specific instructions to help someone. It is important that we respond to those promptings because we never know how much the recipient needs the encouragement or direction God wants us to give.

Joy was the most devastated of all the women in my divorce-recovery class. She had been blindsided by her husband's quick departure, leaving her with three children to raise alone. Yet by the end of the nine-week program she had progressed well beyond anything I could have imagined.

Joy and I stayed in touch and over time she began to date someone. Joy came to a crossroads in that relationship and shared her concerns with me. Since her circumstances were similar to something I had experienced, I felt as if the Lord wanted me to share a Scripture with her that He had given me at my own crossroads. Based upon that prompting, I logged it in my Prayer Closet Organizer and mailed her a card with the Scripture.

A couple of days later Joy called. On the day she received my card, she had told God that very morning that she needed a clear word from Him about her relationship. All throughout her day, she expected to hear from

God. When she got home and opened her mail, there was the word from God tucked in my card. Taking the Scripture to heart, she waited on the Lord. Today, she has a very happy marriage. This is one of the greatest uses of this section: capturing God's instruction.

I am sure that God provided my friend Joy with plenty of other signals that led her to His choice of her future husband, but no one can underestimate the importance of God's intervention through other believers. Are you capturing God's instructions so you can impact the lives of others?

Using the Organizer Helps Defeat the Enemy

When I believe God is asking me to do something, I take some time to pray over it. I like to write it down in my Prayer Closet Organizer, and sometimes I put a question mark at the end of it if I am unsure it is from God. Once I feel clear that God is leading me to do it—when I feel more compelled and perhaps have received some other confirming nudges from Him—I confidently move forward. Sometimes the sense of urgency that I feel about it will just go away, and then I know God has not spoken to me.

This is the beauty of prayer journaling. I can meditate on those things I feel led to do until I am confident that God is speaking to me. When we record God's promptings in our Prayer Closet Organizers, it is like leaving a path of bread crumbs we follow back to God's hand. We can refer to them over and over again as needed for comfort, confirmation, and conclusion. When fear or worry tries to take hold of my mind, I reread what God has spoken to me in a particular situation and am able to regain my peace and hope.

Our enemy, Satan, will sometimes attempt to confuse or deceive us. We can overcome that deception by reviewing what God has spoken directly to us about particular situations in the past. In a unique way, this journal becomes a testimonial.

Revelation 12:11 says that we overcome the enemy by the blood of Jesus and the word of our testimony. The structured format of the Prayer Closet Organizer helps keep our thoughts organized and clear and enables us to quick-reference what God is doing and what He has said He is going to do in our lives. A review of my prayer journal not only fortifies my faith, it also establishes a recognizable pattern of God's direction in my life that I can refer to again when I feel as if He is leading me to do something.

Don't Panic—God Will Help You

If you are in a situation where you are unsure whether you can identify God's voice, don't panic. In God's grace and mercy, He is faithful to try more than once to get our attention. God called out to the little boy Samuel three times before he recognized that the Lord was speaking to him, and only with help from his guardian did he recognize God's voice (see 1 Samuel 3). That is why it is even more crucial to write everything down in this section that you believe may be from God and occasionally to seek counsel from a mentor.

When we journal the impressions we receive from God, we develop ears that hear. It is through the repetitive and consistent practice of structured prayer journaling that I have acquired the discernment to know when God is speaking to me.

Organizing Your Prayer Closet

God speaks to those whose ears are attuned to the Good Shepherd. So many times we cheat ourselves out of listening in prayer. We forward our petitions like e-mail and forget to ask if God would like to say something to us. God has jobs, people, and great opportunities to introduce us to. But we must learn to listen. All throughout Scripture, God spoke to His people—Noah, Moses, David, Paul—about His future plans for them. Thankfully, God has not changed. Like a lamb, you must learn to hear the

Shepherd. There are no shortcuts. You begin with the basics and learn to hear from heaven. You can start by asking yourself these questions and putting your answers in your organizer:

- At any point today, did I feel prompted to encourage someone (call, send a card, visit)?
- Have I felt led to do something, such as read a specific chapter in the Bible or attend an upcoming conference?
- Did the Holy Spirit illuminate any verse during my daily Bible reading today that really spoke to me about a particular situation?
- Is there any situation in which I need to ask counsel from a mentor? If so, when will I do that?

For this department, I list anything I feel God is leading me to do, as well as anything I feel that God is personally speaking to me. Here are some examples of my entries:

EARS TO HEAR
What is God
saying to me?

*"Whatever you do, whether in
speech or action, do it all in the name
of the Lord Jesus and give thanks to
God the Father through him."*
—Colossians 3:17

* Use Ecclesiastes 8:5 as my new rule of thumb
* Volunteer to teach the children's mission class
* Visit Bella's sick mother - have prayer and share
  Scripture

My prayer may sound something like this:

Precious Father, thank You for Ecclesiastes 8:5. I want the wise heart You describe in that Scripture. I want to know how to discern the right procedure and timing for everything You ask me to do. When I heard a recent sermon preached on Samson's misuse and waste of his supernatural strength [Judges 13–16], I felt you strike a chord in my spirit reminding me not to squander what You have given me. I want You to know that I heard You prompting me to teach the children's mission class in that message, Lord. May I always be found being steadfast and faithful in my walk and ministry. God, I am going to visit Bella's sick mother and share the Scriptures You have given me. Thank you for teaching me how to pray for her.

Proceed with much prayer,
and your way will be made plain.
—John Wesley[2]

CHAPTER 11
FAITH AND
FOLLOW-THROUGH

Since you know these things, you will be happy if you do them.
—John 13:17

From all my years of prayer journaling, I have realized that God asks of me far less than I ask of Him. While I may present as many as ten different scenarios to God that need His intervention or guidance every week, He may prompt me to do only a couple of things for Him. It may be as easy as inviting someone to church or as difficult as addressing sin in a friend's life. Even though I obviously prefer the simple requests, I have experienced growth in humility and maturity when I stretch myself to follow through with God's more complicated requests.

It is in the section of Faith and Follow-Through that I will list the date on which I followed up with God's request of me. This section is the Part B to Ears That Hear. Listing my dates of accomplishment helps me easily identify what requests are outstanding.

I understand God expects me to be responsive to those requests that require immediate action. For example, if I were commissioned to give godly counsel to a friend who is having marital problems, I must act in a timely manner: I know I've been nudged at an appointed time, and that may be the time my friend is open to hearing from God. Delaying my response to God on my friend's behalf makes it harder for me to recall the exact words God was leading me to share, and the opportunity for deeper impact may be lessened or gone.

Other times I know I need to wait for an opening or specific time before I am to follow through.

Sometimes my Lord nudges me to do something that seems too challenging for me. But God's eyes see further than my eyes, and because of that His plans do not always make sense to me. When we follow through with God's requests, we feel His grace and peace even when the road is difficult. On the flip side, when we disobey we will not necessarily experience the same grace, mercy, and protection. A good example is the preacher named Jonah who decided to run away from the city that God wanted him to speak to. When he fled God's will he found himself in a storm, thrown off a boat, and in the belly of a fish. Our failure to follow God's lead can take us places we do not want to go. Has this ever happened to you?

The response of follow-through comes from our faith. In order to have faith and follow-through, it is important to develop a strong comfort level in your ability to hear God clearly. Unless we have faith to believe that God is directing us in a particular direction or leading us to do something specific, we will lack the confidence to complete the task. The good news is that practice in follow-through makes perfect faith. Our case study for this truth is in the account of Abraham's journey.

Abraham's Faith and Follow-Through

"The LORD said to Abram, 'Leave your land, your family, and your father's household for the land that I will show you. I will make of you a great nation and will bless you. I will make your name respected, and you will be a blessing'" (Genesis 12:1-2).

Few of us will receive as tall of an order from the Lord as this. God told Abram, as was his name at the time, to take his wife and leave the rest of his family to go somewhere that God would show him. Today, people called to the mission field not only have other missionaries to reference and support systems back home, but they typically also know to what land the Lord is leading them. Not so for Abram. With the assurance that God had spoken, he packed up and left home, but not without a slight deviation: "Abram left just as the LORD told him, and Lot went with him" (Genesis 12:4).

Did you catch it? It does not necessarily say that Abram invited Lot along; however, he did allow his nephew to join him. If the Lord had never said for Abram to leave his family, the third wheel may not have been a big deal, but the fact that God specifically instructed Abram not to take his family made this a very big deal. God designs the plan. God is in control of everything around us. Even when God's instruction does not make sense to our human minds, it does not mean that the instruction is flawed, so it is important we do not ignore or devalue it.

Maybe Abram did not pay much attention to the details of the instruction. Maybe Abram did not think letting Lot go along would be a big deal. These are common thoughts we have as finite beings. What harm could come from allowing Lot to join the travelers? Here are just a few issues that presented themselves:

- The land could not hold both Abram and Lot's animals and entourage (Genesis 13:6).
- Lot's men quarreled with Abram's men (Genesis 13:7).
- Lot's family became part of a sinful city (Genesis 13:12-13).
- Abraham had to rescue Lot's family after they were kidnapped (Genesis 14:14-16).
- Lot's wife was turned into a pillar of salt (Genesis19:23-26).
- Lot's daughters committed adultery with him (Genesis 19:30-36).

One deviation led to problems, unnecessary drama, danger and death, and unspeakable sin for Lot and his family. In life, we value those lessons learned from mistakes, but in the spiritual realm, deviations can have serious eternal consequences. When I feel as if God is speaking to me, I try to be as specific as possible when I write down what I believe I hear from Him. Disobedience can bring a huge amount of grief. When tempted to deviate from God's leading, I remember Lot.

Trusting the Lord's Follow-Through

One of the most exciting things God promised Abram was a child of his own. God reassured him, "Your heir will definitely be your very own biological child. . . . Look up at the sky and count the stars if you think you can. . . . This is how many children you will have" (Genesis 15:4-5).

Abram's wife, Sarai, let her faith falter as years passed with no children. So she came up with what she thought was a great idea. She would give her servant girl Hagar to her husband to bear an heir. His response? "Abram did just as Sarai said" (Genesis 16:2). Hagar became pregnant and apparently proud, so she and her son became thorns in Sarai's side.

We must not grow weary or try to make things happen in our strength, for this always creates unintended problems and potential heartache, as it did for Abram. When Sarah, as God renamed her, gave birth to his second son, Isaac—the true heir of God's promise—Abraham (as God renamed him) had to part ways with his first son, Ishmael, whom he loved deeply (Genesis 21).

Abraham loved Ishmael so much that he would have settled for God's will to be done through this son (Genesis 17:17-19). By settling, he was unknowingly requesting to terminate the birth of the nation of Israel; Israel came to exist through the birth of Isaac, and Jesus the Savior was born of that nation. Had Abraham been allowed to settle short of having Isaac, he would have ultimately eliminated himself from the honor of being the great patriarch of Israel and ancestor of the One who came to save the world. Our disinclination to follow through by faith can keep us from experiencing God's greatest blessings and rewards of this life.

So when God shows me a destination, I write it down and review it when my faith begins to wane. Here is what I have learned from my past inability to follow through: no matter how happy I may be with the outcome of a decision where I decided to settle, I am left with the almost unbearable knowledge that it will never compare to the glorious result God had planned.

What long-term, God-given plan has tested your persevering faith? Is a career choice interfering with God's plan for you? Is a well-intentioned friend trying to talk you into settling for a plan inferior to God's? You can have God's best for your life when you move from a failure to follow through to a habit of faith and follow-through!

Lessons Learned

What I love about Abraham, as he came to be called, is that no painful experiences were wasted on him. He learned from his missteps and increasingly made sure not to duplicate them, so there is hope for us. Abraham got better, not only at obeying in faith, but at following through immediately. Maybe God has spoken something to you, yet you hesitate. Could it be that you have even talked yourself out of it? Perhaps you have let others discourage you. Sometimes there are things God speaks to us that would never make sense to anyone else, and all we can do is be faithful to what He calls us to do.

See how Abraham did just that. We read in Genesis 17:22-23: "When God finished speaking to him, God ascended, leaving Abraham alone. Abraham took his son Ishmael, all those born in his household, and all those purchased with his silver—that is, every male in Abraham's household—and he circumcised the flesh of their foreskins that same day, just as God had told him to do."

God delegated what was a very unusual, if not shocking, procedure to Abraham, and then left Abraham alone with his thoughts, concerns, and maybe even bewilderment. Regardless, Abraham obeyed "that same day." I am not quite sure how he assembled the men and shared this new ritual with them, but I can see that the man of God had grown in his faith and become better with follow-through.

Can we say that about ourselves? It is my prayer that as we continue on our journeys, we are becoming better at believing God and being trustworthy to complete any task given. But do we have our limits? Apparently, Abraham matured to the point that he did not. In Genesis 22, Abraham demonstrated that he was willing to be faithful no matter the personal cost, including giving up his son, Isaac. This is why Abraham is a perfect example of maturing in faith and follow-though. He started out a little shaky, but he made a remarkable recovery.

God had faithfully, on numerous occasions, affirmed that Abraham's reward would be great; He's done the same for us. Whether it is obtaining a divine appointment, a ministry position, or an open door for God's message, we get to experience the thrill of following through, participating in, and witnessing God's wonderful plans. This is why we persevere in our journey. By reading Abraham's account, we can see that like him we can learn to become faithful and reach the goals God has set before us.

Throughout our lives, God will give us both extraordinary and ordinary assignments that will have a profound spiritual impact. We must be as faithful with the basic as we are with what seems complex. When we are steadfast to follow through on what seems ordinary, God uses it for the extraordinary. Whatever God speaks to us, we must obey, whatever the cost.

A Rule of Thumb

I like to use Ecclesiastes 8:5 as my rule of thumb in working out God's timing for follow-through: "Whoever keeps a command will meet no harm, and the wise heart knows the right time and the right way." The New International Version of the Bible says it this way: "The wise heart will know the proper time and proper procedure." If I do not yet know how to accomplish something (the proper procedure), then I know it is not the "proper time" to do it. As such, I focus on what I know to do and wait until the path is clear for the rest.

Before I became the director of women's ministry at my church, all of the components had been stand-alone ideas that I did not know how to execute. Nor was there any reason to try to implement them. After I received my assignment in women's ministry, I could see how they all fit together for mobilizing our women in service and ministry; I now had the proper procedure, which meant it was now the proper time. I am thankful that I had written down all of these God-given ideas in my organizer as I received them, which made them much more retrievable when the time was right. Has God given you some ideas? Are you waiting for the proper procedure to be made plain?

Organizing Your Prayer Closet

Throughout the week, God may give us things to do, and it is important that we write them down and note when we have followed through.

Once we are certain that we have heard from the Lord, it takes all the components of faith, proper timing, proper procedure, and perseverance to follow through with God's plans.

When reviewing this department, you may ask yourself:

- Is there anything hindering me from following through with a specific request?
- Do I feel as if I have the full and proper procedure so that I can proceed quickly?
- Do I have any thoughts or results to report from my faith and follow-through experiences? (Record these in your organizer.)

For this section, I jot down all my notes, detailing my follow-through to God's request. Some of my examples have included:

EARS TO HEAR
What is God
saying to me?

"A person's steps are from the LORD."
—Proverbs 20:24

* Restart recruiting business to help subsidize ministry efforts

Send Marsha a letter to initiate reconciliation

"Impact" - 20-13 theme for our Women's Ministry?

FAITH & FOLLOW-THROUGH
How and when did I
respond to God?

*"Whoever keeps a command will meet no
harm, and the wise heart knows the right time
and the right way."*
—Ecclesiastes 8:5

*Launched in July when 2 former colleagues called
and asked me to help them with a search!*

Done, 8/-19

*Confirmed. Today, pastor used this very word
when challenging the staff to find ways for our
congregation to better "impact" our community
this year!*

With my Scripture header, I pray something similar to this:

Lord, thank You for trusting me with Your plans in ministry. God, I so want to respond quickly, especially when You follow through just as You did for reinitiating my recruiting business. This is just one more example of how any success I might think is mine really derives from Your endless grace and mercy. May I not be hindered in any way from doing Your will. Whether my own insecurities or the attacks of the enemy threaten to disrupt Your plans, may my faith rise to every occasion. And I pray that such faith will be rewarded by a positive response from Marsha so that reconciliation will have its day in our friendship. When I am in doubt about Your direction, *thank You for sending me confirmation as You did for the "Impact" theme. I stand amazed to see how You work through Your church. As I list the dates of every endeavor achieved, may I forever give You the glory and honor.*

I have joyfully dedicated my whole life to the object of exemplifying how much may be accomplished by prayer and faith.
—George Müller[1]

NOTES

Introduction

1. http://christian-quotes.ochristian.com/Charles-H.-Brent-Quotes/
2. Borrowed from Lauren Winner, *Mudhouse Sabbath* (Brewster, MA: Paraclete Press, 2003).

Chapter 1

1. E. M. Bounds, *The Essentials of Prayer* (Seaside, OR: Rough Draft Printing, 2013), 12.

Chapter 2

1. http://www.christian-prayer-quotes.christian-attorney.net/

Chapter 3

1. http://christian-quotes.ochristian.com/Overcoming-Quotes/page-2. shtml

Chapter 4

1. Beth Moore, *Praying God's Word* (Nashville: B&H Publishing Group, 2009), 5.

2. http://www.christian-prayer-quotes.christian-attorney.net/

Chapter 5

1. Clarke's Commentary on the Bible, online.

2. http://www.christian-prayer-quotes.christian-attorney.net/

Chapter 6

1. *Matthew Henry's Concise Commentary;* http://biblehub.com/ecclesiastes/3-11.htm

2. http://christian-quotes.ochristian.com/Matthew-Henry-Quotes/ page-5.shtml

Chapter 7

1. http://christian-quotes.ochristian.com/Prayer-Quotes/page-9.shtml

Chapter 8

1. *Barnes' Notes on the Bible,* http://www.bibletools.org/index.cfm/fuseaction/Bible.show/sVerseID/28898/eVerseID/28898/RTD/barnes/version/ nasbe

2. http://christian-quotes.ochristian.com/Prayer-Quotes/page-37.shtml

Chapter 9

1. Herbert Lockyer, *All the Prayers of the Bible* (Grand Rapids, MI: Zondervan, 1959), 79.

2. http://www.christian-prayer-quotes.christian-attorney.net/

Chapter 10

1. Don Matzat, *The Lord Told Me . . . I Think* (Eugene, OR: Harvest House, 1996), 138.

2. http://christian-quotes.ochristian.com/Prayer-Quotes/page-16.shtml

Chapter 11

1. http://christian-quotes.ochristian.com/George-Mueller-Quotes/page-2.shtml

ACKNOWLEDGMENTS

Thank you

To my parents, James and Judy Black:

I am forever indebted to both of you. To my daddy, whose love allowed me to understand my heavenly Father's love. To my mother, whose sacrificial love has been a true picture of the sacrificial work of the cross through Jesus Christ.

To my grandmother, Minnie Bell Black:

In honor of a godly woman whose Christianity was larger than life. I cherish the memories of her years of journaling.

To my friend and mentor, Steve Griffith:

In honor of one of the greatest visionary leaders of the church. Thank you for your faithful counsel and confidence in the ministry God has blessed me with. You are greatly missed.

THE
PRAYER
CLOSET
ORGANIZER

Before you enter into your own prayer closet, review the following summaries for each compartment. Don't forget to refer back to the lists of questions that serve as prompts at the end of each chapter from time to time.

Praise and Thanksgiving. As you begin to organize your prayer closet, survey your day to recount the things that you want to honor God for in praise and thanksgiving.

Freedom and Forgiveness. As you daily consider where you missed the mark, recognize your continual need for God.

Prayer Petitions. Be thoughtful that your petitions are not the only reason you pray. Although it is very important to take your precious needs before the Lord, also remember to offer praise and thanksgiving.

God Answers. Everything belongs to Jesus and is for His good pleasure and plans. As you receive an answer from the Lord, accept it against the backdrop of God's unfailing love, knowledge, and infinite wisdom. It is important to record God's answers in your journal.

At the Right Time. God's timing is perfect. Honor the day God answered your prayer petitions.

My Heart / My Passion. Unburden your heart so you can begin to think beyond yourself and instead to what God is calling you to do for the kingdom work.

Ambassador Notes. Throughout your day, you have so many opportunities to share Jesus with others. Recount them in the Notes.

Insight and Updates. Can you see the hand of God moving? Your prayer requests are not always quickly answered; however, that does not mean that you cannot see the evidence of faith. Take note of what God is doing.

Ears to Hear. God speaks to those whose ears are attuned to the Good Shepherd. Take time during your prayers to listen to what God is saying to you.

Faith and Follow-Through. Take the time to record your prayers when God whispers something in your ear. When you do so, those prayers will be greater because of Him. When your prayers are answered, mark them complete in the Faith and Follow-Through section.

The Prayer Closet Organizer will train you to focus on the higher things of God. Your prayer life will become everything that God intends. Furthermore, you will become the Christian God intends.

Here is how it works:

1. Look at each compartment of the weekly worksheet, one compartment at a time, and reflect on the day.
2. Write down your thoughts in each compartment as they come to you—this is organizing your prayer closet.
3. Using the Scripture headers, pray the Word of God over your input.
4. Repeat daily.
5. Every Sunday, start a new worksheet.
6. Periodically review the past week's worksheets and update to see God's hand moving in your prayers.

Inside each compartment, you will find clarity and practical insights for a disciplined prayer life and Spirit-led life. Enter in.

"The end of everything has come. Therefore, be self-controlled and clear-headed so you can pray." —1 Peter 4:7

PRAISE & THANKSGIVING

What may I praise &
thank God for today?

*"Shout triumphantly to the Lord, all the
earth! Serve the Lord with celebration!
Come before him with shouts of joy!"*
—Psalm 100:1-2

FREEDOM & FORGIVENESS

What am I
struggling with?

*"But the fruit of the Spirit is love, joy, peace,
patience, kindness, goodness, faithfulness,
gentleness, and self-control. There is no law
against things like this."*
—Galatians 5:22-23

PRAYER PETITIONS

What are my
prayer requests?

*"Rejoice always. Pray continually. Give
thanks in every situation because this is God's
will for you in Christ Jesus."*
—1 Thessalonians 5:16-18

MY HEART / MY PASSION

What is going
on with me?

*"Happy are people who have pure hearts,
because they will see God.*
—Matthew 5:8

AMBASSADOR NOTES

Who did I share
Jesus with today?

*"So we are ambassadors who represent
Christ. God is negotiating with you through
us. We beg you as Christ's representatives, 'Be
reconciled to God!'"*
—2 Corinthians 5:20

INSIGHT & UPDATES

What am I seeing God
do with my prayer?

*"The one who searches hearts knows how the
Spirit thinks, because he pleads for the saints
consistent with God's will."*
—Romans 8:27

GOD ANSWERS	AT THE RIGHT TIME	ADDITIONAL NOTES
What is God's answer to my prayer?	When did God answer my prayer?	

"I cry out to you because you answer me."
—Psalm 17:6

"God says, 'When I decide the time is right, I will establish justice just so.'"
—Psalm 75:2

EARS TO HEAR	FAITH & FOLLOW-THROUGH	ADDITIONAL NOTES
What is God saying to me?	How and when did I respond to God?	

"Stay awake, stand firm in your faith, be brave, be strong. Everything should be done in love."
—I Corinthians 16:13-14

"But the love of God is truly perfected in whoever keeps his word. This is how we know we are in him. The one who claims to remain in him ought to live in the same way as he lived."
—I John 2:5-6

PRAISE & THANKSGIVING

What may I praise &
thank God for today?

*"Shout triumphantly to the LORD, all the
earth! Serve the LORD with celebration!
Come before him with shouts of joy!"*
—Psalm 100:1-2

FREEDOM & FORGIVENESS

What am I
struggling with?

*"But the fruit of the Spirit is love, joy, peace,
patience, kindness, goodness, faithfulness,
gentleness, and self-control. There is no law
against things like this."*
—Galatians 5:22-23

PRAYER PETITIONS

What are my
prayer requests?

*"Rejoice always. Pray continually. Give
thanks in every situation because this is God's
will for you in Christ Jesus."*
—1 Thessalonians 5:16-18

MY HEART / MY PASSION

What is going
on with me?

*"Happy are people who have pure hearts,
because they will see God.*
—Matthew 5:8

AMBASSADOR NOTES

Who did I share
Jesus with today?

*"So we are ambassadors who represent
Christ. God is negotiating with you through
us. We beg you as Christ's representatives, 'Be
reconciled to God!'"*
—2 Corinthians 5:20

INSIGHT & UPDATES

What am I seeing God
do with my prayer?

*"The one who searches hearts knows how the
Spirit thinks, because he pleads for the saints
consistent with God's will."*
—Romans 8:27

GOD ANSWERS	AT THE RIGHT TIME	ADDITIONAL NOTES
What is God's answer to my prayer?	When did God answer my prayer?	

"I cry out to you because you answer me."
—Psalm 17:6

"God says, 'When I decide the time is right, I will establish justice just so.'"
—Psalm 75:2

EARS TO HEAR	FAITH & FOLLOW-THROUGH	ADDITIONAL NOTES
What is God saying to me?	How and when did I respond to God?	

"Stay awake, stand firm in your faith, be brave, be strong. Everything should be done in love."
—1 Corinthians 16:13-14

"But the love of God is truly perfected in whoever keeps his word. This is how we know we are in him. The one who claims to remain in him ought to live in the same way as he lived."
—1 John 2:5-6

PRAISE & THANKSGIVING

What may I praise &
thank God for today?

"Shout triumphantly to the LORD, all the earth! Serve the LORD with celebration! Come before him with shouts of joy!"
—Psalm 100:1-2

FREEDOM & FORGIVENESS

What am I
struggling with?

"But the fruit of the Spirit is love, joy, peace, patience, kindness, goodness, faithfulness, gentleness, and self-control. There is no law against things like this."
—Galatians 5:22-23

PRAYER PETITIONS

What are my
prayer requests?

"Rejoice always. Pray continually. Give thanks in every situation because this is God's will for you in Christ Jesus."
—1 Thessalonians 5:16-18

MY HEART / MY PASSION

What is going
on with me?

"Happy are people who have pure hearts, because they will see God.
—Matthew 5:8

AMBASSADOR NOTES

Who did I share
Jesus with today?

"So we are ambassadors who represent Christ. God is negotiating with you through us. We beg you as Christ's representatives, 'Be reconciled to God!'"
—2 Corinthians 5:20

INSIGHT & UPDATES

What am I seeing God
do with my prayer?

"The one who searches hearts knows how the Spirit thinks, because he pleads for the saints, consistent with God's will."
—Romans 8:27

*he end of everything has come. Therefore, be self-controlled and clearheaded so you can pray." —*I Peter 4:7

GOD ANSWERS	AT THE RIGHT TIME	ADDITIONAL NOTES
What is God's answer to my prayer?	When did God answer my prayer?	

"I cry out to you because you answer me."
—Psalm 17:6

"God says, 'When I decide the time is right, I will establish justice just so.'"
—Psalm 75:2

EARS TO HEAR	FAITH & FOLLOW-THROUGH	ADDITIONAL NOTES
What is God saying to me?	How and when did I respond to God?	

"Stay awake, stand firm in your faith, be brave, be strong. Everything should be done in love."
—I Corinthians 16:13-14

"But the love of God is truly perfected in whoever keeps his word. This is how we know we are in him. The one who claims to remain in him ought to live in the same way as he lived."
—I John 2:5-6

Praise & Thanksgiving
What may I praise & thank God for today?

"Shout triumphantly to the LORD, all the earth! Serve the LORD with celebration! Come before him with shouts of joy!"
—Psalm 100:1-2

_____
_____
_____
_____
_____
_____
_____
_____
_____
_____

Freedom & Forgiveness
What am I struggling with?

"But the fruit of the Spirit is love, joy, peace, patience, kindness, goodness, faithfulness, gentleness, and self-control. There is no law against things like this."
—Galatians 5:22-23

_____
_____
_____
_____
_____
_____
_____
_____
_____
_____

Prayer Petitions
What are my prayer requests?

"Rejoice always. Pray continually. Give thanks in every situation because this is God's will for you in Christ Jesus."
—1 Thessalonians 5:16-18

_____
_____
_____
_____
_____
_____
_____
_____
_____
_____

My Heart / My Passion
What is going on with me?

"Happy are people who have pure hearts, because they will see God.
—Matthew 5:8

_____
_____
_____
_____
_____
_____
_____
_____
_____
_____

Ambassador Notes
Who did I share Jesus with today?

"So we are ambassadors who represent Christ. God is negotiating with you through us. We beg you as Christ's representatives, 'Be reconciled to God!'"
—2 Corinthians 5:20

_____
_____
_____
_____
_____
_____
_____
_____
_____
_____

Insight & Updates
What am I seeing God do with my prayer?

"The one who searches hearts knows how the Spirit thinks, because he pleads for the saints consistent with God's will."
—Romans 8:27

_____
_____
_____
_____
_____
_____
_____
_____
_____
_____

"The end of everything has come. Therefore, be self-controlled and clearheaded so you can pray." —I Peter 4:7

GOD ANSWERS	AT THE RIGHT TIME	ADDITIONAL NOTES
What is God's answer to my prayer?	When did God answer my prayer?	

"I cry out to you because you answer me." —Psalm 17:6

"God says, 'When I decide the time is right, I will establish justice just so.'" —Psalm 75:2

EARS TO HEAR	FAITH & FOLLOW-THROUGH	ADDITIONAL NOTES
What is God saying to me?	How and when did I respond to God?	

"Stay awake, stand firm in your faith, be brave, be strong. Everything should be done in love." —I Corinthians 16:13-14

"But the love of God is truly perfected in whoever keeps his word. This is how we know we are in him. The one who claims to remain in him ought to live in the same way as he lived." —I John 2:5-6

PRAISE & THANKSGIVING

What may I praise &
thank God for today?

*"Shout triumphantly to the LORD, all the
earth! Serve the LORD with celebration!
Come before him with shouts of joy!"*
—Psalm 100:1-2

FREEDOM & FORGIVENESS

What am I
struggling with?

*"But the fruit of the Spirit is love, joy, peace,
patience, kindness, goodness, faithfulness,
gentleness, and self-control. There is no law
against things like this."*
—Galatians 5:22-23

PRAYER PETITIONS

What are my
prayer requests?

*"Rejoice always. Pray continually. Give
thanks in every situation because this is God
will for you in Christ Jesus."*
—1 Thessalonians 5:16-18

MY HEART / MY PASSION

What is going
on with me?

*"Happy are people who have pure hearts,
because they will see God.*
—Matthew 5:8

AMBASSADOR NOTES

Who did I share
Jesus with today?

*"So we are ambassadors who represent
Christ. God is negotiating with you through
us. We beg you as Christ's representatives, 'Be
reconciled to God!'"*
—2 Corinthians 5:20

INSIGHT & UPDATES

What am I seeing God
do with my prayer?

*"The one who searches hearts knows how th
Spirit thinks, because he pleads for the sain
consistent with God's will."*
—Romans 8:27

"The end of everything has come. Therefore, be self-controlled and clearheaded so you can pray." —I Peter 4:7

GOD ANSWERS	AT THE RIGHT TIME	ADDITIONAL NOTES
What is God's answer to my prayer?	When did God answer my prayer?	

"I cry out to you because you answer me."
—Psalm 17:6

"God says, 'When I decide the time is right, I will establish justice just so.'"
—Psalm 75:2

EARS TO HEAR	FAITH & FOLLOW-THROUGH	ADDITIONAL NOTES
What is God saying to me?	How and when did I respond to God?	

"Stay awake, stand firm in your faith, be brave, be strong. Everything should be done in love."
—I Corinthians 16:13-14

"But the love of God is truly perfected in whoever keeps his word. This is how we know we are in him. The one who claims to remain in him ought to live in the same way as he lived."
—I John 2:5-6

PRAISE & THANKSGIVING

What may I praise and
thank God for today?

*"Sing praises to God! Sing
praises! Sing praises to our king! Sing
praises because God is king of the whole
world! Sing praises with a song of
instruction!"*
—Psalm 47:6-7

FREEDOM & FORGIVENESS

What am I
struggling with?

*"See to it that nobody enslaves you with phi-
losophy and foolish deception, which conform
to human traditions and the way the world
thinks and acts rather than Christ."*
—Colossians 2:8

PRAYER PETITIONS

What are my
prayer requests?

*"The LORD has listened to my request. The
LORD accepts my prayer."*
—Psalm 6:9

MY HEART / MY PASSION

What is going
on with me?

*"Where your treasure is, there your heart
will be also."*
—Matthew 6:21

AMBASSADOR NOTES

Who did I share
Jesus with today?

*"Let's also think about how to motivate each
other to show love and to do good works."*
—Hebrews 10:24

INSIGHT & UPDATES

What am I seeing God
do with my prayer?

*"So a person should think about us this way,
as servants of Christ and
managers of God's secrets."*
—1 Corinthians 4:1

GOD ANSWERS	AT THE RIGHT TIME	ADDITIONAL NOTES
What is God's answer to my prayer?	When did God answer my prayer?	

"The rock: his acts are perfection! No doubt about it: all his ways are right! He's the faithful God, never deceiving; altogether righteous and true is he."
—Deuteronomy 32:4

"Let's not get tired of doing good, because in time we'll have a harvest if we don't give up."
—Galatians 6:9

EARS TO HEAR	FAITH & FOLLOW-THROUGH	ADDITIONAL NOTES
What is God saying to me?	How and when did I respond to God?	

"But our people should also learn to devote themselves to doing good in order to meet pressing needs so they aren't unproductive."
—Titus 3:14

"I hurry to keep your commandments— I never put it off!"
—Psalm 119:60

PRAISE & THANKSGIVING
What may I praise and thank God for today?

"Sing praises to God! Sing praises! Sing praises to our king! Sing praises because God is king of the whole world! Sing praises with a song of instruction!"
—Psalm 47:6-7

FREEDOM & FORGIVENESS
What am I struggling with?

"See to it that nobody enslaves you with philosophy and foolish deception, which conform to human traditions and the way the world thinks and acts rather than Christ."
—Colossians 2:8

PRAYER PETITIONS
What are my prayer requests?

"The LORD has listened to my request. The LORD accepts my prayer."
—Psalm 6:9

MY HEART / MY PASSION
What is going on with me?

"Where your treasure is, there your heart will be also."
—Matthew 6:21

AMBASSADOR NOTES
Who did I share Jesus with today?

"Let's also think about how to motivate each other to show love and to do good works."
—Hebrews 10:24

INSIGHT & UPDATES
What am I seeing God do with my prayer?

"So a person should think about us this way, as servants of Christ and managers of God's secrets."
—1 Corinthians 4:1

The end of everything has come. Therefore, be self-controlled and clearheaded so you can pray." —1 Peter 4:7

GOD ANSWERS	AT THE RIGHT TIME	ADDITIONAL NOTES
What is God's answer to my prayer?	When did God answer my prayer?	

"The rock: his acts are perfection! No doubt about it: all his ways are right! He's the faithful God, never deceiving; altogether righteous and true is he."
—Deuteronomy 32:4

"Let's not get tired of doing good, because in time we'll have a harvest if we don't give up."
—Galatians 6:9

EARS TO HEAR	FAITH & FOLLOW-THROUGH	ADDITIONAL NOTES
What is God saying to me?	How and when did I respond to God?	

"But our people should also learn to devote themselves to doing good in order to meet pressing needs so they aren't unproductive."
—Titus 3:14

"I hurry to keep your commandments— I never put it off!"
—Psalm 119:60

PRAISE & THANKSGIVING

What may I praise and
thank God for today?

*"Sing praises to God! Sing praises! Sing
praises to our king! Sing praises because God
is king of the whole world! Sing praises with a
song of instruction!"*
—Psalm 47:6-7

_____

_____

_____

_____

_____

_____

_____

_____

FREEDOM & FORGIVENESS

What am I
struggling with?

*"See to it that nobody enslaves you with phi-
losophy and foolish deception, which conform
to human traditions and the way the world
thinks and acts rather than Christ."*
—Colossians 2:8

_____

_____

_____

_____

_____

_____

_____

_____

PRAYER PETITIONS

What are my
prayer requests?

*"The LORD has listened to my request. The
LORD accepts my prayer."*
—Psalm 6:9

_____

_____

_____

_____

_____

_____

_____

_____

MY HEART / MY PASSION

What is going
on with me?

*"Where your treasure is, there your heart
will be also."*
—Matthew 6:21

_____

_____

_____

_____

_____

_____

_____

_____

AMBASSADOR NOTES

Who did I share
Jesus with today?

*"Let's also think about how to motivate each
other to show love and to do good works."*
—Hebrews 10:24

_____

_____

_____

_____

_____

_____

_____

_____

INSIGHT & UPDATES

What am I seeing God
do with my prayer?

*"So a person should think about us this way,
as servants of Christ and
managers of God's secrets."*
—1 Corinthians 4:1

_____

_____

_____

_____

_____

_____

_____

_____

"The end of everything has come. Therefore, be self-controlled and clearheaded so you can pray." —I Peter 4:7

GOD ANSWERS	AT THE RIGHT TIME	ADDITIONAL NOTES
What is God's answer to my prayer?	When did God answer my prayer?	

"The rock: his acts are perfection! No doubt about it: all his ways are right! He's the faithful God, never deceiving; altogether righteous and true is he."
—Deuteronomy 32:4

"Let's not get tired of doing good, because in time we'll have a harvest if we don't give up."
—Galatians 6:9

EARS TO HEAR	FAITH & FOLLOW-THROUGH	ADDITIONAL NOTES
What is God saying to me?	How and when did I respond to God?	

"But our people should also learn to devote themselves to doing good in order to meet pressing needs so they aren't unproductive."
—Titus 3:14

"I hurry to keep your commandments— I never put it off!"
—Psalm 119:60

PRAISE & THANKSGIVING

What may I praise and
thank God for today?

*"Sing praises to God! Sing praises! Sing
praises to our king! Sing praises because God
is king of the whole world! Sing praises with a
song of instruction!"*
—Psalm 47:6-7

FREEDOM & FORGIVENESS

What am I
struggling with?

*"See to it that nobody enslaves you with phi-
losophy and foolish deception, which conform
to human traditions and the way the world
thinks and acts rather than Christ."*
—Colossians 2:8

PRAYER PETITIONS

What are my
prayer requests?

*"The LORD has listened to my request. The
LORD accepts my prayer."*
—Psalm 6:9

MY HEART / MY PASSION

What is going
on with me?

*"Where your treasure is, there your heart
will be also."*
—Matthew 6:21

AMBASSADOR NOTES

Who did I share
Jesus with today?

*"Let's also think about how to motivate each
other to show love and to do good works."*
—Hebrews 10:24

INSIGHT & UPDATES

What am I seeing God
do with my prayer?

*"So a person should think about us this way—
as servants of Christ and
managers of God's secrets."*
—1 Corinthians 4:1

GOD ANSWERS	AT THE RIGHT TIME	ADDITIONAL NOTES
What is God's answer to my prayer?	When did God answer my prayer?	

*'The rock: his acts are perfection! No doubt
bout it: all his ways are right! He's the faith-
ul God, never deceiving; altogether righteous
and true is he."*
—Deuteronomy 32:4

*"Let's not get tired of doing good, because in
time we'll have a harvest if we don't give up."*
—Galatians 6:9

EARS TO HEAR	FAITH & FOLLOW-THROUGH	ADDITIONAL NOTES
What is God saying to me?	How and when did I respond to God?	

*"But our people should also learn to devote
themselves to doing good in order to meet
ressing needs so they aren't unproductive."*
—Titus 3:14

*"I hurry to keep your commandments—
I never put it off!"*
—Psalm 119:60

PRAISE & THANKSGIVING

What may I praise and
thank God for today?

"Sing praises to God! Sing praises! Sing praises to our king! Sing praises because God is king of the whole world! Sing praises with a song of instruction!"
—Psalm 47:6-7

FREEDOM & FORGIVENESS

What am I
struggling with?

"See to it that nobody enslaves you with philosophy and foolish deception, which conform to human traditions and the way the world thinks and acts rather than Christ."
—Colossians 2:8

PRAYER PETITIONS

What are my
prayer requests?

"The LORD has listened to my request. The LORD accepts my prayer."
—Psalm 6:9

MY HEART / MY PASSION

What is going
on with me?

"Where your treasure is, there your heart will be also."
—Matthew 6:21

AMBASSADOR NOTES

Who did I share
Jesus with today?

"Let's also think about how to motivate each other to show love and to do good works."
—Hebrews 10:24

INSIGHT & UPDATES

What am I seeing God
do with my prayer?

"So a person should think about us this way, as servants of Christ and managers of God's secrets."
—1 Corinthians 4:1

The end of everything has come. Therefore, be self-controlled and clearheaded so you can pray." —I Peter 4:7

GOD ANSWERS	AT THE RIGHT TIME	ADDITIONAL NOTES
What is God's answer to my prayer?	When did God answer my prayer?	

"The rock: his acts are perfection! No doubt about it: all his ways are right! He's the faithful God, never deceiving; altogether righteous and true is he."
—Deuteronomy 32:4

"Let's not get tired of doing good, because in time we'll have a harvest if we don't give up."
—Galatians 6:9

EARS TO HEAR	FAITH & FOLLOW-THROUGH	ADDITIONAL NOTES
What is God saying to me?	How and when did I respond to God?	

"But our people should also learn to devote themselves to doing good in order to meet pressing needs so they aren't unproductive."
—Titus 3:14

"I hurry to keep your commandments— I never put it off!"
—Psalm 119:60

PRAISE & THANKSGIVING
What may I praise and thank God for today?

"Your faithful love is priceless, God! Humanity finds refuge in the shadow of your wings."
—Psalm 36:7

_____
_____
_____
_____
_____
_____
_____
_____
_____
_____

FREEDOM & FORGIVENESS
What am I struggling with?

"Now that you have been set free from sin, you have become slaves of righteousness."
—Romans 6:18

_____
_____
_____
_____
_____
_____
_____
_____
_____
_____

PRAYER PETITIONS
What are my prayer requests?

"For this reason, confess your sins to each other and pray for each other so that you may be healed. The prayer of the righteous person is powerful in what it can achieve."
—James 5:16

_____
_____
_____
_____
_____
_____
_____
_____
_____
_____

MY HEART / MY PASSION
What is going on with me?

"God is the one who enables you both to want and to actually live out his good purposes."
—Philippians 2:13

_____
_____
_____
_____
_____
_____
_____
_____
_____
_____

AMBASSADOR NOTES
Who did I share Jesus with today?

"I publicize my own ministry in the hope that somehow I might make my own people jealous and save some of them."
—Romans 11:13-14

_____
_____
_____
_____
_____
_____
_____
_____
_____
_____

INSIGHT & UPDATES
What am I seeing God do with my prayer?

"If we live by the Spirit, let's follow the Spirit."
—Galatians 5:25

_____
_____
_____
_____
_____
_____
_____
_____
_____
_____

"The end of everything has come. Therefore, be self-controlled and clearheaded so you can pray." —I Peter 4:7

| GOD ANSWERS | AT THE RIGHT TIME | ADDITIONAL NOTES |
| What is God's answer to my prayer? | When did God answer my prayer? | |

"Answer me, LORD, for your faithful love is good! Turn to me in your great compassion!"
—Psalm 69:16

"But me? I trust you, LORD! I affirm, 'You are my God.' My future is in your hands."
—Psalm 31:14-15

| EARS TO HEAR | FAITH & FOLLOW-THROUGH | ADDITIONAL NOTES |
| What is God saying to me? | How and when did I respond to God? | |

"Remember prisoners as if you were in prison with them, and people who are mistreated as if you were in their place."
—Hebrews 13:3

"We are constantly praying for you for this: that our God will make you worthy of his calling and accomplish every good desire and faithful work by his power."
—2 Thessalonians I:II

PRAISE & THANKSGIVING	FREEDOM & FORGIVENESS	PRAYER PETITIONS
What may I praise and thank God for today?	What am I struggling with?	What are my prayer requests?

"Your faithful love is priceless, God! Humanity finds refuge in the shadow of your wings."
—Psalm 36:7

"Now that you have been set free from sin, you have become slaves of righteousness."
—Romans 6:18

"For this reason, confess your sins to each other and pray for each other so that you may be healed. The prayer of the righteous person is powerful in what it can achieve."
—James 5:16

MY HEART / MY PASSION	AMBASSADOR NOTES	INSIGHT & UPDATES
What is going on with me?	Who did I share Jesus with today?	What am I seeing God do with my prayer?

"God is the one who enables you both to want and to actually live out his good purposes."
—Philippians 2:13

"I publicize my own ministry in the hope that somehow I might make my own people jealous and save some of them."
—Romans 11:13-14

"If we live by the Spirit, let's follow the Spirit."
—Galatians 5:25

The end of everything has come. Therefore, be self-controlled and clearheaded so you can pray." —I Peter 4:7

GOD ANSWERS	AT THE RIGHT TIME	ADDITIONAL NOTES
What is God's answer to my prayer?	When did God answer my prayer?	

"Answer me, LORD, for your faithful love is good! Turn to me in your great compassion!"
—Psalm 69:16

"But me? I trust you, LORD! I affirm, 'You are my God.' My future is in your hands."
—Psalm 31:14-15

EARS TO HEAR	FAITH & FOLLOW-THROUGH	ADDITIONAL NOTES
What is God saying to me?	How and when did I respond to God?	

"Remember prisoners as if you were in prison with them, and people who are mistreated as if you were in their place."
—Hebrews 13:3

"We are constantly praying for you for this: that our God will make you worthy of his calling and accomplish every good desire and faithful work by his power."
—2 Thessalonians 1:11

PRAISE & THANKSGIVING

What may I praise and
thank God for today?

*"Your faithful love is priceless, God!
Humanity finds refuge in the
shadow of your wings."*
—Psalm 36:7

_____

_____

_____

_____

_____

_____

_____

_____

_____

_____

FREEDOM & FORGIVENESS

What am I
struggling with?

*"Now that you have been set free from sin,
you have become slaves of righteousness."*
—Romans 6:18

_____

_____

_____

_____

_____

_____

_____

_____

_____

_____

PRAYER PETITIONS

What are my
prayer requests?

*"For this reason, confess your sins to each
other and pray for each other so that you m
be healed. The prayer of the righteous perso
is powerful in what it can achieve."*
—James 5:16

_____

_____

_____

_____

_____

_____

_____

_____

_____

_____

MY HEART / MY PASSION

What is going
on with me?

*"God is the one who enables you both to want
and to actually live out his good purposes."*
—Philippians 2:13

_____

_____

_____

_____

_____

_____

_____

_____

_____

_____

AMBASSADOR NOTES

Who did I share
Jesus with today?

*"I publicize my own ministry in the hope that
somehow I might make my own people jealous
and save some of them."*
—Romans 11:13-14

_____

_____

_____

_____

_____

_____

_____

_____

_____

_____

INSIGHT & UPDATES

What am I seeing God
do with my prayer?

*"If we live by the Spirit,
let's follow the Spirit."*
—Galatians 5:25

_____

_____

_____

_____

_____

_____

_____

_____

_____

_____

"The end of everything has come. Therefore, be self-controlled and clearheaded so you can pray." —I Peter 4:7

GOD ANSWERS	AT THE RIGHT TIME	ADDITIONAL NOTES
What is God's answer to my prayer?	When did God answer my prayer?	

"Answer me, Lord, for your faithful love is good! Turn to me in your great compassion!"
—Psalm 69:16

"But me? I trust you, Lord! I affirm, 'You are my God.' My future is in your hands."
—Psalm 31:14-15

EARS TO HEAR	FAITH & FOLLOW-THROUGH	ADDITIONAL NOTES
What is God saying to me?	How and when did I respond to God?	

"Remember prisoners as if you were in prison with them, and people who are mistreated as if you were in their place."
—Hebrews 13:3

"We are constantly praying for you for this: that our God will make you worthy of his calling and accomplish every good desire and faithful work by his power."
—2 Thessalonians 1:11

PRAISE & THANKSGIVING

What may I praise and
thank God for today?

"Your faithful love is priceless, God!
Humanity finds refuge in the
shadow of your wings."
—Psalm 36:7

_____

_____

_____

_____

_____

_____

_____

_____

_____

_____

FREEDOM & FORGIVENESS

What am I
struggling with?

"Now that you have been set free from sin,
you have become slaves of righteousness."
—Romans 6:18

_____

_____

_____

_____

_____

_____

_____

_____

_____

_____

PRAYER PETITIONS

What are my
prayer requests?

"For this reason, confess your sins to each
other and pray for each other so that you may
be healed. The prayer of the righteous person
is powerful in what it can achieve."
—James 5:16

_____

_____

_____

_____

_____

_____

_____

_____

_____

_____

MY HEART / MY PASSION

What is going
on with me?

"God is the one who enables you both to want
and to actually live out his good purposes."
—Philippians 2:13

_____

_____

_____

_____

_____

_____

_____

_____

_____

AMBASSADOR NOTES

Who did I share
Jesus with today?

"I publicize my own ministry in the hope that
somehow I might make my own people jealous
and save some of them."
—Romans 11:13-14

_____

_____

_____

_____

_____

_____

_____

_____

_____

INSIGHT & UPDATES

What am I seeing God
do with my prayer?

"If we live by the Spirit,
let's follow the Spirit."
—Galatians 5:25

_____

_____

_____

_____

_____

_____

_____

_____

_____

"The end of everything has come. Therefore, be self-controlled and clearheaded so you can pray." —I Peter 4:7

GOD ANSWERS	AT THE RIGHT TIME	ADDITIONAL NOTES
What is God's answer to my prayer?	When did God answer my prayer?	

"Answer me, LORD, for your faithful love is good! Turn to me in your great compassion!"
—Psalm 69:16

"But me? I trust you, LORD! I affirm, 'You are my God.' My future is in your hands."
—Psalm 31:14-15

EARS TO HEAR	FAITH & FOLLOW-THROUGH	ADDITIONAL NOTES
What is God saying to me?	How and when did I respond to God?	

"Remember prisoners as if you were in prison with them, and people who are mistreated as if you were in their place."
—Hebrews 13:3

"We are constantly praying for you for this: that our God will make you worthy of his calling and accomplish every good desire and faithful work by his power."
—2 Thessalonians I:II

PRAISE & THANKSGIVING

What may I praise and
thank God for today?

*"Your faithful love is priceless, God!
Humanity finds refuge in the
shadow of your wings."*
—Psalm 36:7

_____

_____

_____

_____

_____

_____

_____

_____

_____

FREEDOM & FORGIVENESS

What am I
struggling with?

*"Now that you have been set free from sin,
you have become slaves of righteousness."*
—Romans 6:18

_____

_____

_____

_____

_____

_____

_____

_____

_____

PRAYER PETITIONS

What are my
prayer requests?

*"For this reason, confess your sins to each
other and pray for each other so that you may
be healed. The prayer of the righteous person
is powerful in what it can achieve."*
—James 5:16

_____

_____

_____

_____

_____

_____

_____

_____

_____

MY HEART / MY PASSION

What is going
on with me?

*"God is the one who enables you both to want
and to actually live out his good purposes."*
—Philippians 2:13

_____

_____

_____

_____

_____

_____

_____

_____

_____

AMBASSADOR NOTES

Who did I share
Jesus with today?

*"I publicize my own ministry in the hope that
somehow I might make my own people jealous
and save some of them."*
—Romans 11:13-14

_____

_____

_____

_____

_____

_____

_____

_____

_____

INSIGHT & UPDATES

What am I seeing God
do with my prayer?

*"If we live by the Spirit,
let's follow the Spirit."*
—Galatians 5:25

_____

_____

_____

_____

_____

_____

_____

_____

_____

'The end of everything has come. Therefore, be self-controlled and clearheaded so you can pray." —1 Peter 4:7

GOD ANSWERS	AT THE RIGHT TIME	ADDITIONAL NOTES
What is God's answer to my prayer?	When did God answer my prayer?	

"Answer me, LORD, for your faithful love is good! Turn to me in your great compassion!"
—Psalm 69:16

"But me? I trust you, LORD! I affirm, 'You are my God.' My future is in your hands."
—Psalm 31:14-15

EARS TO HEAR	FAITH & FOLLOW-THROUGH	ADDITIONAL NOTES
What is God saying to me?	How and when did I respond to God?	

"Remember prisoners as if you were in prison with them, and people who are mistreated as if you were in their place."
—Hebrews 13:3

"We are constantly praying for you for this: that our God will make you worthy of his calling and accomplish every good desire and faithful work by his power."
—2 Thessalonians 1:11

PRAISE & THANKSGIVING

What may I praise and
thank God for today?

*"But don't be ashamed if you suffer as one
who belongs to Christ. Rather, honor God as
you bear Christ's name. Give honor to God."*
—1 Peter 4:16

_____
_____
_____
_____
_____
_____
_____
_____
_____

FREEDOM & FORGIVENESS

What am I
struggling with?

*"My child, don't make light of the Lord's
discipline or give up when you are corrected by
him, because the Lord disciplines whomever
he loves, and he punishes every son or daughter whom he accepts."*
—Hebrews 12:5-6

_____
_____
_____
_____
_____
_____
_____
_____
_____

PRAYER PETITIONS

What are my
prayer requests?

*"And I tell you: Ask and you will receive. S
and you will find. Knock and the door will
opened to you. Everyone who asks, receiv
Whoever seeks, finds. To everyone who
knocks, the door is opened."*
—Luke 11:9-10

_____
_____
_____
_____
_____
_____
_____
_____
_____

MY HEART / MY PASSION

What is going
on with me?

*"I want to do your will, my God. Your
Instruction is deep within me."*
—Psalm 40:8

_____
_____
_____
_____
_____
_____
_____
_____
_____

AMBASSADOR NOTES

Who did I share
Jesus with today?

*"I thank Christ Jesus our Lord, who has given
me strength because he considered me faithful.
So he appointed me to ministry."*
—1 Timothy 1:12

_____
_____
_____
_____
_____
_____
_____
_____
_____

INSIGHT & UPDATES

What am I seeing God
do with my prayer?

*"And yes, you want truth in the most hid
places; you teach me wisdom
in the most secret space."*
—Psalm 51:6

_____
_____
_____
_____
_____
_____
_____
_____
_____

"The end of everything has come. Therefore, be self-controlled and clearheaded so you can pray." —I Peter 4:7

GOD ANSWERS	AT THE RIGHT TIME	ADDITIONAL NOTES
What is God's answer to my prayer?	When did God answer my prayer?	

"The LORD will do all this for my sake. Your faithful love lasts forever, LORD! Don't let go of what your hands have made."
—Psalm 138:8

"God has made everything fitting in its time, but has also placed eternity in their hearts, without enabling them to discover what God has done from beginning to end."
—Ecclesiastes 3:11

EARS TO HEAR	FAITH & FOLLOW-THROUGH	ADDITIONAL NOTES
What is God saying to me?	How and when did I respond to God?	

"Think about the things above and not things on earth."
—Colossians 3:2

"See to it that you complete the ministry that you received in the Lord."
—Colossians 4:17

PRAISE & THANKSGIVING

What may I praise and
thank God for today?

*"But don't be ashamed if you suffer as one
who belongs to Christ. Rather, honor God as
you bear Christ's name. Give honor to God."*
—1 Peter 4:16

FREEDOM & FORGIVENESS

What am I
struggling with?

*"My child, don't make light of the Lord's
discipline or give up when you are corrected by
him, because the Lord disciplines whomever
he loves, and he punishes every son or daughter whom he accepts."*
—Hebrews 12:5-6

PRAYER PETITIONS

What are my
prayer requests?

*"And I tell you: Ask and you will receive. Se
and you will find. Knock and the door will
opened to you. Everyone who asks, receive
Whoever seeks, finds. To everyone who
knocks, the door is opened."*
—Luke 11:9-10

MY HEART / MY PASSION

What is going
on with me?

*"I want to do your will, my God. Your
Instruction is deep within me."*
—Psalm 40:8

AMBASSADOR NOTES

Who did I share
Jesus with today?

*"I thank Christ Jesus our Lord, who has given
me strength because he considered me faithful.
So he appointed me to ministry."*
—1 Timothy 1:12

INSIGHT & UPDATES

What am I seeing God
do with my prayer?

*"And yes, you want truth in the most hidd
places; you teach me wisdom
in the most secret space."*
—Psalm 51:6

"The end of everything has come. Therefore, be self-controlled and clearheaded so you can pray." —I Peter 4:7

GOD ANSWERS	AT THE RIGHT TIME	ADDITIONAL NOTES
What is God's answer to my prayer?	When did God answer my prayer?	

"The LORD will do all this for my sake. Your faithful love lasts forever, LORD! Don't let go of what your hands have made."
—Psalm 138:8

"God has made everything fitting in its time, but has also placed eternity in their hearts, without enabling them to discover what God has done from beginning to end."
—Ecclesiastes 3:11

EARS TO HEAR	FAITH & FOLLOW-THROUGH	ADDITIONAL NOTES
What is God saying to me?	How and when did I respond to God?	

"Think about the things above and not things on earth."
—Colossians 3:2

"See to it that you complete the ministry that you received in the Lord."
—Colossians 4:17

PRAISE & THANKSGIVING

What may I praise and
thank God for today?

*"But don't be ashamed if you suffer as one
who belongs to Christ. Rather, honor God as
you bear Christ's name. Give honor to God."*
—1 Peter 4:16

_____
_____
_____
_____
_____
_____
_____
_____
_____

FREEDOM & FORGIVENESS

What am I
struggling with?

*"My child, don't make light of the Lord's
discipline or give up when you are corrected by
him, because the Lord disciplines whomever
he loves, and he punishes every son or daughter whom he accepts."*
—Hebrews 12:5-6

_____
_____
_____
_____
_____
_____
_____
_____
_____

PRAYER PETITIONS

What are my
prayer requests?

*"And I tell you: Ask and you will receive. Seek
and you will find. Knock and the door will be
opened to you. Everyone who asks, receives.
Whoever seeks, finds. To everyone who
knocks, the door is opened."*
—Luke 11:9-10

_____
_____
_____
_____
_____
_____
_____
_____
_____

MY HEART / MY PASSION

What is going
on with me?

*"I want to do your will, my God. Your
Instruction is deep within me."*
—Psalm 40:8

_____
_____
_____
_____
_____
_____
_____
_____
_____

AMBASSADOR NOTES

Who did I share
Jesus with today?

*"I thank Christ Jesus our Lord, who has given
me strength because he considered me faithful.
So he appointed me to ministry."*
—1 Timothy 1:12

_____
_____
_____
_____
_____
_____
_____
_____
_____

INSIGHT & UPDATES

What am I seeing God
do with my prayer?

*"And yes, you want truth in the most hidden
places; you teach me wisdom
in the most secret space."*
—Psalm 51:6

_____
_____
_____
_____
_____
_____
_____
_____
_____

"The end of everything has come. Therefore, be self-controlled and clearheaded so you can pray." —1 Peter 4:7

GOD ANSWERS	AT THE RIGHT TIME	ADDITIONAL NOTES
What is God's answer to my prayer?	When did God answer my prayer?	

"The LORD will do all this for my sake. Your faithful love lasts forever, LORD! Don't let go of what your hands have made."
—Psalm 138:8

"God has made everything fitting in its time, but has also placed eternity in their hearts, without enabling them to discover what God has done from beginning to end."
—Ecclesiastes 3:11

EARS TO HEAR	FAITH & FOLLOW-THROUGH	ADDITIONAL NOTES
What is God saying to me?	How and when did I respond to God?	

"Think about the things above and not things on earth."
—Colossians 3:2

"See to it that you complete the ministry that you received in the Lord."
—Colossians 4:17

PRAISE & THANKSGIVING	FREEDOM & FORGIVENESS	PRAYER PETITIONS
What may I praise and thank God for today?	What am I struggling with?	What are my prayer requests?

"But don't be ashamed if you suffer as one who belongs to Christ. Rather, honor God as you bear Christ's name. Give honor to God."
—1 Peter 4:16

"My child, don't make light of the Lord's discipline or give up when you are corrected by him, because the Lord disciplines whomever he loves, and he punishes every son or daughter whom he accepts."
—Hebrews 12:5-6

"And I tell you: Ask and you will receive. Se and you will find. Knock and the door will opened to you. Everyone who asks, receive Whoever seeks, finds. To everyone who knocks, the door is opened."
—Luke 11:9-10

MY HEART / MY PASSION	AMBASSADOR NOTES	INSIGHT & UPDATES
What is going on with me?	Who did I share Jesus with today?	What am I seeing God do with my prayer?

"I want to do your will, my God. Your Instruction is deep within me."
—Psalm 40:8

"I thank Christ Jesus our Lord, who has given me strength because he considered me faithful. So he appointed me to ministry."
—1 Timothy 1:12

"And yes, you want truth in the most hidde places; you teach me wisdom in the most secret space."
—Psalm 51:6

GOD ANSWERS	AT THE RIGHT TIME	ADDITIONAL NOTES
What is God's answer to my prayer?	When did God answer my prayer?	

"The LORD will do all this for my sake. Your faithful love lasts forever, LORD! Don't let go of what your hands have made."
—Psalm 138:8

"God has made everything fitting in its time, but has also placed eternity in their hearts, without enabling them to discover what God has done from beginning to end."
—Ecclesiastes 3:11

EARS TO HEAR	FAITH & FOLLOW-THROUGH	ADDITIONAL NOTES
What is God saying to me?	How and when did I respond to God?	

"Think about the things above and not things on earth."
—Colossians 3:2

"See to it that you complete the ministry that you received in the Lord."
—Colossians 4:17

PRAISE & THANKSGIVING

What may I praise and thank God for today?

"But don't be ashamed if you suffer as one who belongs to Christ. Rather, honor God as you bear Christ's name. Give honor to God."
—1 Peter 4:16

_____

_____

_____

_____

_____

_____

_____

_____

_____

FREEDOM & FORGIVENESS

What am I struggling with?

"My child, don't make light of the Lord's discipline or give up when you are corrected by him, because the Lord disciplines whomever he loves, and he punishes every son or daughter whom he accepts."
—Hebrews 12:5-6

_____

_____

_____

_____

_____

_____

_____

_____

_____

PRAYER PETITIONS

What are my prayer requests?

"And I tell you: Ask and you will receive. and you will find. Knock and the door wil opened to you. Everyone who asks, recei Whoever seeks, finds. To everyone wh knocks, the door is opened."
—Luke 11:9-10

_____

_____

_____

_____

_____

_____

_____

_____

_____

MY HEART / MY PASSION

What is going on with me?

"I want to do your will, my God. Your Instruction is deep within me."
—Psalm 40:8

_____

_____

_____

_____

_____

_____

_____

_____

AMBASSADOR NOTES

Who did I share Jesus with today?

"I thank Christ Jesus our Lord, who has given me strength because he considered me faithful. So he appointed me to ministry."
—1 Timothy 1:12

_____

_____

_____

_____

_____

_____

_____

_____

INSIGHT & UPDATES

What am I seeing God do with my prayer?

"And yes, you want truth in the most hid places; you teach me wisdom in the most secret space."
—Psalm 51:6

_____

_____

_____

_____

_____

_____

_____

_____

"The end of everything has come. Therefore, be self-controlled and clearheaded so you can pray." —I Peter 4:7

GOD ANSWERS	AT THE RIGHT TIME	ADDITIONAL NOTES
What is God's answer to my prayer?	When did God answer my prayer?	

"The LORD will do all this for my sake. Your faithful love lasts forever, LORD! Don't let go of what your hands have made."
—Psalm 138:8

"God has made everything fitting in its time, but has also placed eternity in their hearts, without enabling them to discover what God has done from beginning to end."
—Ecclesiastes 3:11

EARS TO HEAR	FAITH & FOLLOW-THROUGH	ADDITIONAL NOTES
What is God saying to me?	How and when did I respond to God?	

"Think about the things above and not things on earth."
—Colossians 3:2

"See to it that you complete the ministry that you received in the Lord."
—Colossians 4:17

PRAISE & THANKSGIVING

What may I praise and
thank God for today?

*"May the God and Father of our Lord Jesus
Christ be blessed! He is the compassionate
Father and God of all comfort."*
—2 Corinthians 1:3

FREEDOM & FORGIVENESS

What am I
struggling with?

*"Therefore, submit to God. Resist the devil,
and he will run away from you."*
—James 4:7

PRAYER PETITIONS

What are my
prayer requests?

*"Cry out to me whenever you are in trouble; I
will deliver you, then you will honor me."*
—Psalm 50:15

MY HEART / MY PASSION

What is going
on with me?

"A marvelous word has stirred my heart."
—Psalm 45:1

AMBASSADOR NOTES

Who did I share
Jesus with today?

*"Serve each other according to the gift each
person has received, as good managers of
God's diverse gifts."*
—1 Peter 4:10

INSIGHT & UPDATES

What am I seeing God
do with my prayer?

*"God has revealed his hidden design to us,
which is according to his goodwill
and the plan that he intended to
accomplish through his son."*
—Ephesians 1:9

*The end of everything has come. Therefore, be self-controlled and clearheaded so you can pray." —*I Peter 4:7

GOD ANSWERS	AT THE RIGHT TIME	ADDITIONAL NOTES
What is God's answer to my prayer?	When did God answer my prayer?	

"It is impossible to please God without faith because the one who draws near to God must believe that he exists and that he rewards people who try to find him."
—Hebrews 11:6

"This is what God planned for the climax of all times: to bring all things together in Christ, the things in heaven along with the things of the earth."
—Ephesians 1:10

EARS TO HEAR	FAITH & FOLLOW-THROUGH	ADDITIONAL NOTES
What is God saying to me?	How and when did I respond to God?	

"Once you have your minds ready for action and you are thinking clearly, place your hope completely on the grace that will be brought to you when Jesus Christ is revealed."
—I Peter 1:13

"Now finish the job as well so that you finish it with as much enthusiasm as you started."
—2 Corinthians 8:11

PRAISE & THANKSGIVING

What may I praise and thank God for today?

"May the God and Father of our Lord Jesus Christ be blessed! He is the compassionate Father and God of all comfort."
—2 Corinthians 1:3

FREEDOM & FORGIVENESS

What am I struggling with?

"Therefore, submit to God. Resist the devil, and he will run away from you."
—James 4:7

PRAYER PETITIONS

What are my prayer requests?

"Cry out to me whenever you are in trouble, will deliver you, then you will honor me."
—Psalm 50:15

MY HEART / MY PASSION

What is going on with me?

"A marvelous word has stirred my heart."
—Psalm 45:1

AMBASSADOR NOTES

Who did I share Jesus with today?

"Serve each other according to the gift each person has received, as good managers of God's diverse gifts."
—1 Peter 4:10

INSIGHT & UPDATES

What am I seeing God do with my prayer?

"God has revealed his hidden design to us which is according to his goodwill and the plan that he intended to accomplish through his son."
—Ephesians 1:9

"The end of everything has come. Therefore, be self-controlled and clearheaded so you can pray." —I Peter 4:7

GOD ANSWERS	AT THE RIGHT TIME	ADDITIONAL NOTES
What is God's answer to my prayer?	When did God answer my prayer?	

"It is impossible to please God without faith because the one who draws near to God must believe that he exists and that he rewards people who try to find him."
—Hebrews 11:6

"This is what God planned for the climax of all times: to bring all things together in Christ, the things in heaven along with the things of the earth."
—Ephesians 1:10

EARS TO HEAR	FAITH & FOLLOW-THROUGH	ADDITIONAL NOTES
What is God saying to me?	How and when did I respond to God?	

"Once you have your minds ready for action and you are thinking clearly, place your hope completely on the grace that will be brought to you when Jesus Christ is revealed."
—I Peter 1:13

"Now finish the job as well so that you finish it with as much enthusiasm as you started."
—2 Corinthians 8:11

Week _____

*"May the God and Father of our Lord Jesus
Christ be blessed! He is the compassionate
Father and God of all comfort."*
—2 Corinthians 1:3

*"Therefore, submit to God. Resist the devil,
and he will run away from you."*
—James 4:7

*"Cry out to me whenever you are in troub
will deliver you, then you will honor me*
—Psalm 50:15

"A marvelous word has stirred my heart."
—Psalm 45:1

*"Serve each other according to the gift each
person has received, as good managers of
God's diverse gifts."*
—1 Peter 4:10

*"God has revealed his hidden design to
which is according to his goodwill
and the plan that he intended to
accomplish through his son."*
—Ephesians 1:9

"The end of everything has come. Therefore, be self-controlled and clearheaded so you can pray." —1 Peter 4:7

GOD ANSWERS	AT THE RIGHT TIME	ADDITIONAL NOTES
What is God's answer to my prayer?	When did God answer my prayer?	

"It is impossible to please God without faith because the one who draws near to God must believe that he exists and that he rewards people who try to find him."
—Hebrews 11:6

"This is what God planned for the climax of all times: to bring all things together in Christ, the things in heaven along with the things of the earth."
—Ephesians 1:10

EARS TO HEAR	FAITH & FOLLOW-THROUGH	ADDITIONAL NOTES
What is God saying to me?	How and when did I respond to God?	

"Once you have your minds ready for action and you are thinking clearly, place your hope completely on the grace that will be brought to you when Jesus Christ is revealed."
—1 Peter 1:13

"Now finish the job as well so that you finish it with as much enthusiasm as you started."
—2 Corinthians 8:11

PRAISE & THANKSGIVING

What may I praise and
thank God for today?

"May the God and Father of our Lord Jesus
Christ be blessed! He is the compassionate
Father and God of all comfort."
—2 Corinthians 1:3

_____
_____
_____
_____
_____
_____
_____
_____
_____
_____
_____

FREEDOM & FORGIVENESS

What am I
struggling with?

"Therefore, submit to God. Resist the devil,
and he will run away from you."
—James 4:7

_____
_____
_____
_____
_____
_____
_____
_____
_____
_____
_____

PRAYER PETITIONS

What are my
prayer requests?

"Cry out to me whenever you are in trouble; I
will deliver you, then you will honor me."
—Psalm 50:15

_____
_____
_____
_____
_____
_____
_____
_____
_____
_____
_____

MY HEART / MY PASSION

What is going
on with me?

"A marvelous word has stirred my heart."
—Psalm 45:1

_____
_____
_____
_____
_____
_____
_____
_____

AMBASSADOR NOTES

Who did I share
Jesus with today?

"Serve each other according to the gift each
person has received, as good managers of
God's diverse gifts."
—1 Peter 4:10

_____
_____
_____
_____
_____
_____
_____
_____

INSIGHT & UPDATES

What am I seeing God
do with my prayer?

"God has revealed his hidden design to us,
which is according to his goodwill
and the plan that he intended to
accomplish through his son."
—Ephesians 1:9

_____
_____
_____
_____
_____
_____
_____
_____

GOD ANSWERS	AT THE RIGHT TIME	ADDITIONAL NOTES
What is God's answer to my prayer?	When did God answer my prayer?	

"It is impossible to please God without faith because the one who draws near to God must believe that he exists and that he rewards people who try to find him."
—Hebrews 11:6

"This is what God planned for the climax of all times: to bring all things together in Christ, the things in heaven along with the things of the earth."
—Ephesians 1:10

EARS TO HEAR	FAITH & FOLLOW-THROUGH	ADDITIONAL NOTES
What is God saying to me?	How and when did I respond to God?	

"Once you have your minds ready for action and you are thinking clearly, place your hope completely on the grace that will be brought to you when Jesus Christ is revealed."
—I Peter 1:13

"Now finish the job as well so that you finish it with as much enthusiasm as you started."
—2 Corinthians 8:11

PRAISE & THANKSGIVING

What may I praise and
thank God for today?

*"May the God and Father of our Lord Jesus
Christ be blessed! He is the compassionate
Father and God of all comfort."*
—2 Corinthians 1:3

_____
_____
_____
_____
_____
_____
_____
_____
_____

FREEDOM & FORGIVENESS

What am I
struggling with?

*"Therefore, submit to God. Resist the devil,
and he will run away from you."*
—James 4:7

_____
_____
_____
_____
_____
_____
_____
_____
_____

PRAYER PETITIONS

What are my
prayer requests?

*"Cry out to me whenever you are in troub
will deliver you, then you will honor me.*
—Psalm 50:15

_____
_____
_____
_____
_____
_____
_____
_____
_____

MY HEART / MY PASSION

What is going
on with me?

"A marvelous word has stirred my heart."
—Psalm 45:1

_____
_____
_____
_____
_____
_____
_____
_____

AMBASSADOR NOTES

Who did I share
Jesus with today?

*"Serve each other according to the gift each
person has received, as good managers of
God's diverse gifts."*
—1 Peter 4:10

_____
_____
_____
_____
_____
_____
_____
_____

INSIGHT & UPDATES

What am I seeing God
do with my prayer?

*"God has revealed his hidden design to u
which is according to his goodwill
and the plan that he intended to
accomplish through his son."*
—Ephesians 1:9

_____
_____
_____
_____
_____
_____
_____
_____

GOD ANSWERS	AT THE RIGHT TIME	ADDITIONAL NOTES
What is God's answer to my prayer?	When did God answer my prayer?	

"It is impossible to please God without faith because the one who draws near to God must believe that he exists and that he rewards people who try to find him."
—Hebrews 11:6

"This is what God planned for the climax of all times: to bring all things together in Christ, the things in heaven along with the things of the earth."
—Ephesians 1:10

EARS TO HEAR	FAITH & FOLLOW-THROUGH	ADDITIONAL NOTES
What is God saying to me?	How and when did I respond to God?	

"Once you have your minds ready for action and you are thinking clearly, place your hope completely on the grace that will be brought to you when Jesus Christ is revealed."
—1 Peter 1:13

"Now finish the job as well so that you finish it with as much enthusiasm as you started."
—2 Corinthians 8:11

PRAISE & THANKSGIVING

What may I praise and
thank God for today?

*"Our Lord is great and so strong! God's
knowledge can't be grasped!"*
—Psalm 147:5

FREEDOM & FORGIVENESS

What am I
struggling with?

*"If those who claim devotion to God don't
control what they say, they mislead themselves. Their devotion is worthless."*
—James 1:26

PRAYER PETITIONS

What are my
prayer requests?

*"LORD, let your ear be attentive . . . to the
prayer of your servants who delight in honoring your name. Please give success to your
servant today and grant him favor."*
—Nehemiah 1:11

MY HEART / MY PASSION

What is going
on with me?

*"Scatter your seed in the morning, and in
the evening don't be idle because you don't
know which will succeed, this one or that, or
whether both will be equally good."*
—Ecclesiastes 11:6

AMBASSADOR NOTES

Who did I share
Jesus with today?

*"Make sure no one misses out on God's grace.
Make sure that no root of bitterness grows up
that might cause trouble and pollute many
people."*
—Hebrews 12:15

INSIGHT & UPDATES

What am I seeing God
do with my prayer?

*"But anyone who needs wisdom should ask
God, whose very nature is to give to everyone
without a second thought, without keeping
score. Wisdom will certainly be given to
those who ask."*
—James 1:5

"The end of everything has come. Therefore, be self-controlled and clearheaded so you can pray." —I Peter 4:7

GOD ANSWERS	AT THE RIGHT TIME	ADDITIONAL NOTES
What is God's answer to my prayer?	When did God answer my prayer?	

"We have also received an inheritance in Christ. We were destined by the plan of God, who accomplishes everything according to his design."
—Ephesians I:II

"The Lord isn't slow to keep his promise, as some think of slowness, but he is patient toward you, not wanting anyone to perish but all to change their hearts and lives."
—2 Peter 3:9

EARS TO HEAR	FAITH & FOLLOW-THROUGH	ADDITIONAL NOTES
What is God saying to me?	How and when did I respond to God?	

"Don't be conformed to the patterns of this world, but be transformed by the renewing of your minds so that you can figure out what God's will is—what is good and pleasing and mature."
—Romans I2:2

"I have been crucified with Christ and I no longer live, but Christ lives in me. And the life I now live in my body, I live by faith, indeed, by faithfulness of God's Son, who loved me and gave himself for me."
—Galatians 2:20

PRAISE & THANKSGIVING

What may I praise and
thank God for today?

*"Our Lord is great and so strong! God's
knowledge can't be grasped!"*
—Psalm 147:5

FREEDOM & FORGIVENESS

What am I
struggling with?

*"If those who claim devotion to God don't
control what they say, they mislead themselves. Their devotion is worthless."*
—James 1:26

PRAYER PETITIONS

What are my
prayer requests?

*"LORD, let your ear be attentive . . . to the
prayer of your servants who delight in honoring your name. Please give success to your
servant today and grant him favor."*
—Nehemiah 1:11

MY HEART / MY PASSION

What is going
on with me?

*"Scatter your seed in the morning, and in
the evening don't be idle because you don't
know which will succeed, this one or that, or
whether both will be equally good."*
—Ecclesiastes 11:6

AMBASSADOR NOTES

Who did I share
Jesus with today?

*"Make sure no one misses out on God's grace.
Make sure that no root of bitterness grows up
that might cause trouble and pollute many
people."*
—Hebrews 12:15

INSIGHT & UPDATES

What am I seeing God
do with my prayer?

*"But anyone who needs wisdom should ask
God, whose very nature is to give to everyon
without a second thought, without keeping
score. Wisdom will certainly be given to
those who ask."*
—James 1:5

'The end of everything has come. Therefore, be self-controlled and clearheaded so you can pray." —1 Peter 4:7

GOD ANSWERS	AT THE RIGHT TIME	ADDITIONAL NOTES
What is God's answer to my prayer?	When did God answer my prayer?	

"We have also received an inheritance in Christ. We were destined by the plan of God, who accomplishes everything according to his design."
—Ephesians 1:11

"The Lord isn't slow to keep his promise, as some think of slowness, but he is patient toward you, not wanting anyone to perish but all to change their hearts and lives."
—2 Peter 3:9

EARS TO HEAR	FAITH & FOLLOW-THROUGH	ADDITIONAL NOTES
What is God saying to me?	How and when did I respond to God?	

"Don't be conformed to the patterns of this world, but be transformed by the renewing of your minds so that you can figure out what God's will is—what is good and pleasing and mature."
—Romans 12:2

"I have been crucified with Christ and I no longer live, but Christ lives in me. And the life I now live in my body, I live by faith, indeed, by faithfulness of God's Son, who loved me and gave himself for me."
—Galatians 2:20

PRAISE & THANKSGIVING

What may I praise and thank God for today?

"Our Lord is great and so strong! God's knowledge can't be grasped!"
—Psalm 147:5

_____

_____

_____

_____

_____

_____

_____

_____

_____

_____

FREEDOM & FORGIVENESS

What am I struggling with?

"If those who claim devotion to God don't control what they say, they mislead themselves. Their devotion is worthless."
—James 1:26

_____

_____

_____

_____

_____

_____

_____

_____

_____

_____

PRAYER PETITIONS

What are my prayer requests?

"Lord, let your ear be attentive . . . to the prayer of your servants who delight in honoring your name. Please give success to your servant today and grant him favor."
—Nehemiah 1:11

_____

_____

_____

_____

_____

_____

_____

_____

_____

_____

MY HEART / MY PASSION

What is going on with me?

"Scatter your seed in the morning, and in the evening don't be idle because you don't know which will succeed, this one or that, or whether both will be equally good."
—Ecclesiastes 11:6

_____

_____

_____

_____

_____

_____

_____

_____

_____

AMBASSADOR NOTES

Who did I share Jesus with today?

"Make sure no one misses out on God's grace. Make sure that no root of bitterness grows up that might cause trouble and pollute many people."
—Hebrews 12:15

_____

_____

_____

_____

_____

_____

_____

_____

_____

INSIGHT & UPDATES

What am I seeing God do with my prayer?

"But anyone who needs wisdom should ask God, whose very nature is to give to everyone without a second thought, without keeping score. Wisdom will certainly be given to those who ask."
—James 1:5

_____

_____

_____

_____

_____

_____

_____

_____

_____

"The end of everything has come. Therefore, be self-controlled and clearheaded so you can pray." —1 Peter 4:7

GOD ANSWERS	AT THE RIGHT TIME	ADDITIONAL NOTES
What is God's answer to my prayer?	When did God answer my prayer?	

"We have also received an inheritance in Christ. We were destined by the plan of God, who accomplishes everything according to his design."
—Ephesians 1:11

"The Lord isn't slow to keep his promise, as some think of slowness, but he is patient toward you, not wanting anyone to perish but all to change their hearts and lives."
—2 Peter 3:9

EARS TO HEAR	FAITH & FOLLOW-THROUGH	ADDITIONAL NOTES
What is God saying to me?	How and when did I respond to God?	

"Don't be conformed to the patterns of this world, but be transformed by the renewing of your minds so that you can figure out what God's will is—what is good and pleasing and mature."
—Romans 12:2

"I have been crucified with Christ and I no longer live, but Christ lives in me. And the life I now live in my body, I live by faith, indeed, by faithfulness of God's Son, who loved me and gave himself for me."
—Galatians 2:20

PRAISE & THANKSGIVING

What may I praise and
thank God for today?

*"Our Lord is great and so strong! God's
knowledge can't be grasped!"*
—Psalm 147:5

_____

_____

_____

_____

_____

_____

_____

_____

_____

_____

FREEDOM & FORGIVENESS

What am I
struggling with?

*"If those who claim devotion to God don't
control what they say, they mislead themselves. Their devotion is worthless."*
—James 1:26

_____

_____

_____

_____

_____

_____

_____

_____

_____

_____

PRAYER PETITIONS

What are my
prayer requests?

*"LORD, let your ear be attentive . . . to the
prayer of your servants who delight in honoring your name. Please give success to your
servant today and grant him favor."*
—Nehemiah 1:11

_____

_____

_____

_____

_____

_____

_____

_____

_____

_____

MY HEART / MY PASSION

What is going
on with me?

*"Scatter your seed in the morning, and in
the evening don't be idle because you don't
know which will succeed, this one or that, or
whether both will be equally good."*
—Ecclesiastes 11:6

_____

_____

_____

_____

_____

_____

_____

_____

_____

AMBASSADOR NOTES

Who did I share
Jesus with today?

*"Make sure no one misses out on God's grace.
Make sure that no root of bitterness grows up
that might cause trouble and pollute many
people."*
—Hebrews 12:15

_____

_____

_____

_____

_____

_____

_____

_____

_____

INSIGHT & UPDATES

What am I seeing God
do with my prayer?

*"But anyone who needs wisdom should ask
God, whose very nature is to give to everyone
without a second thought, without keeping
score. Wisdom will certainly be given to
those who ask."*
—James 1:5

_____

_____

_____

_____

_____

_____

_____

_____

_____

"The end of everything has come. Therefore, be self-controlled and clearheaded so you can pray." —I Peter 4:7

GOD ANSWERS	AT THE RIGHT TIME	ADDITIONAL NOTES
What is God's answer to my prayer?	When did God answer my prayer?	

"We have also received an inheritance in Christ. We were destined by the plan of God, who accomplishes everything according to his design."
—Ephesians 1:11

"The Lord isn't slow to keep his promise, as some think of slowness, but he is patient toward you, not wanting anyone to perish but all to change their hearts and lives."
—2 Peter 3:9

EARS TO HEAR	FAITH & FOLLOW-THROUGH	ADDITIONAL NOTES
What is God saying to me?	How and when did I respond to God?	

"Don't be conformed to the patterns of this world, but be transformed by the renewing of your minds so that you can figure out what God's will is—what is good and pleasing and mature."
—Romans 12:2

"I have been crucified with Christ and I no longer live, but Christ lives in me. And the life I now live in my body, I live by faith, indeed, by faithfulness of God's Son, who loved me and gave himself for me."
—Galatians 2:20

PRAISE & THANKSGIVING

What may I praise and
thank God for today?

*"Our Lord is great and so strong! God's
knowledge can't be grasped!"*
—Psalm 147:5

_____

_____

_____

_____

_____

_____

_____

_____

_____

_____

FREEDOM & FORGIVENESS

What am I
struggling with?

*"If those who claim devotion to God don't
control what they say, they mislead themselves. Their devotion is worthless."*
—James 1:26

PRAYER PETITIONS

What are my
prayer requests?

*"LORD, let your ear be attentive . . . to the
prayer of your servants who delight in honoring your name. Please give success to your
servant today and grant him favor."*
—Nehemiah 1:11

MY HEART / MY PASSION

What is going
on with me?

*"Scatter your seed in the morning, and in
the evening don't be idle because you don't
know which will succeed, this one or that, or
whether both will be equally good."*
—Ecclesiastes 11:6

AMBASSADOR NOTES

Who did I share
Jesus with today?

*"Make sure no one misses out on God's grace.
Make sure that no root of bitterness grows up
that might cause trouble and pollute many
people."*
—Hebrews 12:15

INSIGHT & UPDATES

What am I seeing God
do with my prayer?

*"But anyone who needs wisdom should ask
God, whose very nature is to give to everyone
without a second thought, without keeping
score. Wisdom will certainly be given to
those who ask."*
—James 1:5

The end of everything has come. Therefore, be self-controlled and clearheaded so you can pray." —I Peter 4:7

GOD ANSWERS	AT THE RIGHT TIME	ADDITIONAL NOTES
What is God's answer to my prayer?	When did God answer my prayer?	

"We have also received an inheritance in Christ. We were destined by the plan of God, who accomplishes everything according to his design."
—Ephesians 1:11

"The Lord isn't slow to keep his promise, as some think of slowness, but he is patient toward you, not wanting anyone to perish but all to change their hearts and lives."
—2 Peter 3:9

EARS TO HEAR	FAITH & FOLLOW-THROUGH	ADDITIONAL NOTES
What is God saying to me?	How and when did I respond to God?	

"Don't be conformed to the patterns of this world, but be transformed by the renewing of your minds so that you can figure out what God's will is—what is good and pleasing and mature."
—Romans 12:2

"I have been crucified with Christ and I no longer live, but Christ lives in me. And the life I now live in my body, I live by faith, indeed, by faithfulness of God's Son, who loved me and gave himself for me."
—Galatians 2:20

PRAISE & THANKSGIVING	FREEDOM & FORGIVENESS	PRAYER PETITIONS
What may I praise and thank God for today?	What am I struggling with?	What are my prayer requests?

"Bless the God and Father of the Lord Jesus Christ! He has blessed us in Christ with every spiritual blessing that comes from heaven."
—Ephesians 1:3

"So now there isn't any condemnation for those who are in Christ Jesus. The law of the Spirit of life in Christ Jesus has set you free from the law of sin and death."
—Romans 8:1-2

"Throw all your anxiety onto him, because he cares about you."
—1 Peter 5:7

MY HEART / MY PASSION	AMBASSADOR NOTES	INSIGHT & UPDATES
What is going on with me?	Who did I share Jesus with today?	What am I seeing God do with my prayer?

"Let God grant what is in your heart and fulfill all your plans."
—Psalm 20:4

"The word of Christ must live in you richly. Teach and warn each other with all wisdom by singing psalms, hymns, and spiritual songs. Sing to God with gratitude in your hearts."
—Colossians 3:16

"Good insight brings favor, but the way of the faithless is their ruin."
—Proverbs 13:15

'The end of everything has come. Therefore, be self-controlled and clearheaded so you can pray." —I Peter 4:7

GOD ANSWERS	AT THE RIGHT TIME	ADDITIONAL NOTES
What is God's answer to my prayer?	When did God answer my prayer?	

"Let's draw near to the throne of favor with confidence so that we can receive mercy and find grace when we need help."
—Hebrews 4:16

"Your eyes saw my embryo, and on your scroll every day was written that was being formed for me, before any one of them had yet happened."
—Psalm 139:16

EARS TO HEAR	FAITH & FOLLOW-THROUGH	ADDITIONAL NOTES
What is God saying to me?	How and when did I respond to God?	

"As a result of all this, my dear brothers and sisters, you must stand firm, unshakable, excelling in the work of the Lord as always, because you know that your labor isn't going to be for nothing in the Lord."
—I Corinthians 15:58

"There's a season for everything and a time for every matter under the heavens."
—Ecclesiastes 3:1

PRAISE & THANKSGIVING

What may I praise and
thank God for today?

*"Bless the God and Father of the Lord Jesus
Christ! He has blessed us in Christ with every
spiritual blessing that comes from heaven."*
—Ephesians 1:3

FREEDOM & FORGIVENESS

What am I
struggling with?

*"So now there isn't any condemnation for
those who are in Christ Jesus. The law of the
Spirit of life in Christ Jesus has set you free
from the law of sin and death."*
—Romans 8:1-2

PRAYER PETITIONS

What are my
prayer requests?

*"Throw all your anxiety onto him, because he
cares about you."*
—1 Peter 5:7

MY HEART / MY PASSION

What is going
on with me?

*"Let God grant what is in your heart and
fulfill all your plans."*
—Psalm 20:4

AMBASSADOR NOTES

Who did I share
Jesus with today?

*"The word of Christ must live in you richly.
Teach and warn each other with all wisdom
by singing psalms, hymns, and spiritual songs.
Sing to God with gratitude in your hearts."*
—Colossians 3:16

INSIGHT & UPDATES

What am I seeing God
do with my prayer?

*"Good insight brings favor, but the way
of the faithless is their ruin."*
—Proverbs 13:15

"The end of everything has come. Therefore, be self-controlled and clearheaded so you can pray." —I Peter 4:7

| GOD ANSWERS | AT THE RIGHT TIME | ADDITIONAL NOTES |
What is God's answer to my prayer?	When did God answer my prayer?	
"Let's draw near to the throne of favor with confidence so that we can receive mercy and find grace when we need help." —Hebrews 4:16	*"Your eyes saw my embryo, and on your scroll every day was written that was being formed for me, before any one of them had yet happened."* —Psalm 139:16	

| EARS TO HEAR | FAITH & FOLLOW-THROUGH | ADDITIONAL NOTES |
What is God saying to me?	How and when did I respond to God?	
"As a result of all this, my dear brothers and sisters, you must stand firm, unshakable, excelling in the work of the Lord as always, because you know that your labor isn't going to be for nothing in the Lord." —I Corinthians 15:58	*"There's a season for everything and a time for every matter under the heavens."* —Ecclesiastes 3:1	

PRAISE & THANKSGIVING

What may I praise and
thank God for today?

"Bless the God and Father of the Lord Jesus Christ! He has blessed us in Christ with every spiritual blessing that comes from heaven."
—Ephesians 1:3

FREEDOM & FORGIVENESS

What am I
struggling with?

"So now there isn't any condemnation for those who are in Christ Jesus. The law of the Spirit of life in Christ Jesus has set you free from the law of sin and death."
—Romans 8:1-2

PRAYER PETITIONS

What are my
prayer requests?

"Throw all your anxiety onto him, because he cares about you."
—1 Peter 5:7

MY HEART / MY PASSION

What is going
on with me?

"Let God grant what is in your heart and fulfill all your plans."
—Psalm 20:4

AMBASSADOR NOTES

Who did I share
Jesus with today?

"The word of Christ must live in you richly. Teach and warn each other with all wisdom by singing psalms, hymns, and spiritual songs. Sing to God with gratitude in your hearts."
—Colossians 3:16

INSIGHT & UPDATES

What am I seeing God
do with my prayer?

"Good insight brings favor, but the way of the faithless is their ruin."
—Proverbs 13:15

GOD ANSWERS	AT THE RIGHT TIME	ADDITIONAL NOTES
What is God's answer to my prayer?	When did God answer my prayer?	

"Let's draw near to the throne of favor with confidence so that we can receive mercy and find grace when we need help."
—Hebrews 4:16

"Your eyes saw my embryo, and on your scroll every day was written that was being formed for me, before any one of them had yet happened."
—Psalm 139:16

EARS TO HEAR	FAITH & FOLLOW-THROUGH	ADDITIONAL NOTES
What is God saying to me?	How and when did I respond to God?	

"As a result of all this, my dear brothers and sisters, you must stand firm, unshakable, excelling in the work of the Lord as always, because you know that your labor isn't going to be for nothing in the Lord."
—I Corinthians 15:58

"There's a season for everything and a time for every matter under the heavens."
—Ecclesiastes 3:1

PRAISE & THANKSGIVING

What may I praise and
thank God for today?

*"Bless the God and Father of the Lord Jesus
Christ! He has blessed us in Christ with every
spiritual blessing that comes from heaven."*
—Ephesians 1:3

_____

_____

_____

_____

_____

_____

_____

_____

_____

_____

FREEDOM & FORGIVENESS

What am I
struggling with?

*"So now there isn't any condemnation for
those who are in Christ Jesus. The law of the
Spirit of life in Christ Jesus has set you free
from the law of sin and death."*
—Romans 8:1-2

_____

_____

_____

_____

_____

_____

_____

_____

_____

_____

PRAYER PETITIONS

What are my
prayer requests?

*"Throw all your anxiety onto him, because
cares about you."*
—1 Peter 5:7

_____

_____

_____

_____

_____

_____

_____

_____

_____

_____

MY HEART / MY PASSION

What is going
on with me?

*"Let God grant what is in your heart and
fulfill all your plans."*
—Psalm 20:4

_____

_____

_____

_____

_____

_____

_____

_____

_____

AMBASSADOR NOTES

Who did I share
Jesus with today?

*"The word of Christ must live in you richly.
Teach and warn each other with all wisdom
by singing psalms, hymns, and spiritual songs.
Sing to God with gratitude in your hearts."*
—Colossians 3:16

_____

_____

_____

_____

_____

_____

_____

_____

_____

INSIGHT & UPDATES

What am I seeing God
do with my prayer?

*"Good insight brings favor, but the way
of the faithless is their ruin."*
—Proverbs 13:15

_____

_____

_____

_____

_____

_____

_____

_____

_____

The end of everything has come. Therefore, be self-controlled and clearheaded so you can pray." —I Peter 4:7

GOD ANSWERS
What is God's answer
to my prayer?

"Let's draw near to the throne of favor with confidence so that we can receive mercy and find grace when we need help."
—Hebrews 4:16

AT THE RIGHT TIME
When did God
answer my prayer?

"Your eyes saw my embryo, and on your scroll every day was written that was being formed for me, before any one of them had yet happened."
—Psalm 139:16

ADDITIONAL NOTES

EARS TO HEAR
What is God
saying to me?

"As a result of all this, my dear brothers and sisters, you must stand firm, unshakable, excelling in the work of the Lord as always, because you know that your labor isn't going to be for nothing in the Lord."
—I Corinthians 15:58

FAITH & FOLLOW-THROUGH
How and when did I
respond to God?

"There's a season for everything and a time for every matter under the heavens."
—Ecclesiastes 3:1

ADDITIONAL NOTES

Week _____

PRAISE & THANKSGIVING
What may I praise and thank God for today?

"Bless the God and Father of the Lord Jesus Christ! He has blessed us in Christ with every spiritual blessing that comes from heaven."
—Ephesians 1:3

_____
_____
_____
_____
_____
_____
_____
_____
_____
_____

FREEDOM & FORGIVENESS
What am I struggling with?

"So now there isn't any condemnation for those who are in Christ Jesus. The law of the Spirit of life in Christ Jesus has set you free from the law of sin and death."
—Romans 8:1-2

_____
_____
_____
_____
_____
_____
_____
_____
_____
_____

PRAYER PETITIONS
What are my prayer requests?

"Throw all your anxiety onto him, because cares about you."
—1 Peter 5:7

_____
_____
_____
_____
_____
_____
_____
_____
_____
_____

MY HEART / MY PASSION
What is going on with me?

"Let God grant what is in your heart and fulfill all your plans."
—Psalm 20:4

_____
_____
_____
_____
_____
_____
_____
_____
_____

AMBASSADOR NOTES
Who did I share Jesus with today?

"The word of Christ must live in you richly. Teach and warn each other with all wisdom by singing psalms, hymns, and spiritual songs. Sing to God with gratitude in your hearts."
—Colossians 3:16

_____
_____
_____
_____
_____
_____
_____
_____
_____

INSIGHT & UPDATES
What am I seeing God do with my prayer?

"Good insight brings favor, but the way of the faithless is their ruin."
—Proverbs 13:15

_____
_____
_____
_____
_____
_____
_____
_____
_____

"The end of everything has come. Therefore, be self-controlled and clearheaded so you can pray." —I Peter 4:7

GOD ANSWERS	AT THE RIGHT TIME	ADDITIONAL NOTES
What is God's answer to my prayer?	When did God answer my prayer?	

"Let's draw near to the throne of favor with confidence so that we can receive mercy and find grace when we need help."
—Hebrews 4:16

"Your eyes saw my embryo, and on your scroll every day was written that was being formed for me, before any one of them had yet happened."
—Psalm 139:16

EARS TO HEAR	FAITH & FOLLOW-THROUGH	ADDITIONAL NOTES
What is God saying to me?	How and when did I respond to God?	

"As a result of all this, my dear brothers and sisters, you must stand firm, unshakable, excelling in the work of the Lord as always, because you know that your labor isn't going to be for nothing in the Lord."
—I Corinthians 15:58

"There's a season for everything and a time for every matter under the heavens."
—Ecclesiastes 3:1

PRAISE & THANKSGIVING

What may I praise and
thank God for today?

*"You changed my mourning into dancing. You
took off my funeral clothes and dressed me
up in joy so that my whole being might sing
praises to you and never stop. LORD, my God,
I will give thanks to you forever."*
—Psalm 30:11-12

_____

_____

_____

_____

_____

_____

_____

_____

_____

_____

FREEDOM & FORGIVENESS

What am I
struggling with?

*"The person that we used to be was
crucified with him in order to get rid of the
corpse that had been controlled by sin . . .
because a person who has died has
been freed from sin's power."*
—Romans 6:6-7

_____

_____

_____

_____

_____

_____

_____

_____

_____

_____

PRAYER PETITIONS

What are my
prayer requests?

*"The LORD is close to everyone who calls out t
him, to all who call out to him sincerely."*
—Psalm 145:18

_____

_____

_____

_____

_____

_____

_____

_____

_____

_____

MY HEART / MY PASSION

What is going
on with me?

*"Therefore, if you were raised with Christ,
look for the things that are above where Christ
is sitting at God's right side."*
—Colossians 3:1

_____

_____

_____

_____

_____

_____

_____

_____

AMBASSADOR NOTES

Who did I share
Jesus with today?

*"The Lord has anointed me. He has sent me
to preach good news to the poor, to proclaim
release to the prisoners and recovery of sight to
the blind, to liberate the oppressed."*
—Luke 4:18

_____

_____

_____

_____

_____

_____

_____

_____

INSIGHT & UPDATES

What am I seeing God
do with my prayer?

*"The secret things belong to the LORD our
God. The revealed things belong to us."*
—Deuteronomy 29:29

_____

_____

_____

_____

_____

_____

_____

_____

'The end of everything has come. Therefore, be self-controlled and clearheaded so you can pray." —I Peter 4:7

GOD ANSWERS	AT THE RIGHT TIME	ADDITIONAL NOTES
What is God's answer to my prayer?	When did God answer my prayer?	

"Jesus replied, 'What is impossible for humans is possible for God.'"
—Luke 18:27

"Jesus replied, 'It isn't for you to know the times or seasons that the Father has set by his own authority.'"
—Acts 1:7

EARS TO HEAR	FAITH & FOLLOW-THROUGH	ADDITIONAL NOTES
What is God saying to me?	How and when did I respond to God?	

"More than anything you guard, protect your mind, for life flows from it."
—Proverbs 4:23

"You know that the testing of your faith produces endurance."
—James 1:3

PRAISE & THANKSGIVING

What may I praise and
thank God for today?

*"You changed my mourning into dancing. You
took off my funeral clothes and dressed me
up in joy so that my whole being might sing
praises to you and never stop. LORD, my God,
I will give thanks to you forever."*
—Psalm 30:11-12

FREEDOM & FORGIVENESS

What am I
struggling with?

*"The person that we used to be was
crucified with him in order to get rid of the
corpse that had been controlled by sin . . .
because a person who has died has
been freed from sin's power."*
—Romans 6:6-7

PRAYER PETITIONS

What are my
prayer requests?

*"The LORD is close to everyone who calls out to
him, to all who call out to him sincerely."*
—Psalm 145:18

MY HEART / MY PASSION

What is going
on with me?

*"Therefore, if you were raised with Christ,
look for the things that are above where Christ
is sitting at God's right side."*
—Colossians 3:1

AMBASSADOR NOTES

Who did I share
Jesus with today?

*"The Lord has anointed me. He has sent me
to preach good news to the poor, to proclaim
release to the prisoners and recovery of sight to
the blind, to liberate the oppressed."*
—Luke 4:18

INSIGHT & UPDATES

What am I seeing God
do with my prayer?

*"The secret things belong to the LORD our
God. The revealed things belong to us."*
—Deuteronomy 29:29

*"The end of everything has come. Therefore, be self-controlled and clearheaded so you can pray." —*I Peter 4:7

GOD ANSWERS	AT THE RIGHT TIME	ADDITIONAL NOTES
What is God's answer to my prayer?	When did God answer my prayer?	

"Jesus replied, 'What is impossible for humans is possible for God.'"
—Luke 18:27

"Jesus replied, 'It isn't for you to know the times or seasons that the Father has set by his own authority.'"
—Acts 1:7

EARS TO HEAR	FAITH & FOLLOW-THROUGH	ADDITIONAL NOTES
What is God saying to me?	How and when did I respond to God?	

"More than anything you guard, protect your mind, for life flows from it."
—Proverbs 4:23

"You know that the testing of your faith produces endurance."
—James 1:3

Week _____

"You changed my mourning into dancing. You took off my funeral clothes and dressed me up in joy so that my whole being might sing praises to you and never stop. LORD, my God, I will give thanks to you forever."
—Psalm 30:11-12

"The person that we used to be was crucified with him in order to get rid of the corpse that had been controlled by sin . . . because a person who has died has been freed from sin's power."
—Romans 6:6-7

"The LORD is close to everyone who calls out to him, to all who call out to him sincerely."
—Psalm 145:18

"Therefore, if you were raised with Christ, look for the things that are above where Christ is sitting at God's right side."
—Colossians 3:1

"The Lord has anointed me. He has sent me to preach good news to the poor, to proclaim release to the prisoners and recovery of sight to the blind, to liberate the oppressed."
—Luke 4:18

"The secret things belong to the LORD our God. The revealed things belong to us."
—Deuteronomy 29:29

"The end of everything has come. Therefore, be self-controlled and clearheaded so you can pray." —1 Peter 4:7

GOD ANSWERS	AT THE RIGHT TIME	ADDITIONAL NOTES
What is God's answer to my prayer?	When did God answer my prayer?	

"Jesus replied, 'What is impossible for humans is possible for God.'"
—Luke 18:27

"Jesus replied, 'It isn't for you to know the times or seasons that the Father has set by his own authority.'"
—Acts 1:7

EARS TO HEAR	FAITH & FOLLOW-THROUGH	ADDITIONAL NOTES
What is God saying to me?	How and when did I respond to God?	

"More than anything you guard, protect your mind, for life flows from it."
—Proverbs 4:23

"You know that the testing of your faith produces endurance."
—James 1:3

PRAISE & THANKSGIVING

What may I praise and
thank God for today?

*"You changed my mourning into dancing. You
took off my funeral clothes and dressed me
up in joy so that my whole being might sing
praises to you and never stop. LORD, my God,
I will give thanks to you forever."*
—Psalm 30:11-12

FREEDOM & FORGIVENESS

What am I
struggling with?

*"The person that we used to be was
crucified with him in order to get rid of the
corpse that had been controlled by sin . . .
because a person who has died has
been freed from sin's power."*
—Romans 6:6-7

PRAYER PETITIONS

What are my
prayer requests?

*"The LORD is close to everyone who calls out to
him, to all who call out to him sincerely."*
—Psalm 145:18

MY HEART / MY PASSION

What is going
on with me?

*"Therefore, if you were raised with Christ,
look for the things that are above where Christ
is sitting at God's right side."*
—Colossians 3:1

AMBASSADOR NOTES

Who did I share
Jesus with today?

*"The Lord has anointed me. He has sent me
to preach good news to the poor, to proclaim
release to the prisoners and recovery of sight to
the blind, to liberate the oppressed."*
—Luke 4:18

INSIGHT & UPDATES

What am I seeing God
do with my prayer?

*"The secret things belong to the LORD our
God. The revealed things belong to us."*
—Deuteronomy 29:29

"The end of everything has come. Therefore, be self-controlled and clearheaded so you can pray." —I Peter 4:7

GOD ANSWERS	AT THE RIGHT TIME	ADDITIONAL NOTES
What is God's answer to my prayer?	When did God answer my prayer?	

"Jesus replied, 'What is impossible for humans is possible for God.'"
—Luke 18:27

"Jesus replied, 'It isn't for you to know the times or seasons that the Father has set by his own authority.'"
—Acts 1:7

EARS TO HEAR	FAITH & FOLLOW-THROUGH	ADDITIONAL NOTES
What is God saying to me?	How and when did I respond to God?	

"More than anything you guard, protect your mind, for life flows from it."
—Proverbs 4:23

"You know that the testing of your faith produces endurance."
—James 1:3

PRAISE & THANKSGIVING

What may I praise and thank God for today?

"You changed my mourning into dancing. You took off my funeral clothes and dressed me up in joy so that my whole being might sing praises to you and never stop. LORD, my God, I will give thanks to you forever."
—Psalm 30:11-12

FREEDOM & FORGIVENESS

What am I struggling with?

"The person that we used to be was crucified with him in order to get rid of the corpse that had been controlled by sin . . . because a person who has died has been freed from sin's power."
—Romans 6:6-7

PRAYER PETITIONS

What are my prayer requests?

"The LORD is close to everyone who calls out him, to all who call out to him sincerely."
—Psalm 145:18

MY HEART / MY PASSION

What is going on with me?

"Therefore, if you were raised with Christ, look for the things that are above where Christ is sitting at God's right side."
—Colossians 3:1

AMBASSADOR NOTES

Who did I share Jesus with today?

"The Lord has anointed me. He has sent me to preach good news to the poor, to proclaim release to the prisoners and recovery of sight to the blind, to liberate the oppressed."
—Luke 4:18

INSIGHT & UPDATES

What am I seeing God do with my prayer?

"The secret things belong to the LORD our God. The revealed things belong to us."
—Deuteronomy 29:29

The end of everything has come. Therefore, be self-controlled and clearheaded so you can pray." —I Peter 4:7

GOD ANSWERS	AT THE RIGHT TIME	ADDITIONAL NOTES
What is God's answer to my prayer?	When did God answer my prayer?	

'Jesus replied, 'What is impossible for humans is possible for God.'"
—Luke 18:27

"Jesus replied, 'It isn't for you to know the times or seasons that the Father has set by his own authority.'"
—Acts 1:7

EARS TO HEAR	FAITH & FOLLOW-THROUGH	ADDITIONAL NOTES
What is God saying to me?	How and when did I respond to God?	

"More than anything you guard, protect your mind, for life flows from it."
—Proverbs 4:23

"You know that the testing of your faith produces endurance."
—James 1:3

Week _____

PRAISE & THANKSGIVING

What may I praise and
thank God for today?

*"Bless the Lord! The God of our salvation
supports us day after day!"*
—Psalm 68:19

_____
_____
_____
_____
_____
_____
_____
_____
_____
_____

FREEDOM & FORGIVENESS

What am I
struggling with?

*"Be encouraged, my child, your sins are
forgiven."*
—Matthew 9:2

_____
_____
_____
_____
_____
_____
_____
_____
_____
_____

PRAYER PETITIONS

What are my
prayer requests?

*"Don't be anxious about anything; rather, br
up all your requests to God in your prayers a
petitions, along with giving thanks."*
—Philippians 4:6

_____
_____
_____
_____
_____
_____
_____
_____
_____
_____

MY HEART / MY PASSION

What is going
on with me?

*"We are God's accomplishment, created in
Christ Jesus to do good things.
God planned these good things to be the way
that we live our lives."*
—Ephesians 2:10

_____
_____
_____
_____
_____
_____
_____
_____

AMBASSADOR NOTES

Who did I share
Jesus with today?

*"Preach the word. Be ready to do it whether it
is convenient or inconvenient.
Correct, confront, and encourage with
patience and instruction."*
—2 Timothy 4:2

_____
_____
_____
_____
_____
_____
_____
_____

INSIGHT & UPDATES

What am I seeing God
do with my prayer?

*"What of the wisdom from above?
First, it is pure, and then peaceful, gentle
obedient, filled with mercy and
good actions, fair and genuine."*
—James 3:17

_____
_____
_____
_____
_____
_____
_____
_____

"The end of everything has come. Therefore, be self-controlled and clearheaded so you can pray." —I Peter 4:7

GOD ANSWERS	AT THE RIGHT TIME	ADDITIONAL NOTES
What is God's answer to my prayer?	When did God answer my prayer?	

"We know that God works all things together for good for the ones who love God, for those who are called according to his purpose." —Romans 8:28

"Keep alert, because you don't know the day or the hour." —Matthew 25:13

EARS TO HEAR	FAITH & FOLLOW-THROUGH	ADDITIONAL NOTES
What is God saying to me?	How and when did I respond to God?	

"Focus on working on your own development and on what you teach. If you do this, you will save yourself and those who hear you." —I Timothy 4:16

"Much will be demanded from everyone who has been given much, and from the one who has been entrusted with much, even more will be asked." —Luke 12:48

PRAISE & THANKSGIVING

What may I praise and
thank God for today?

*"Bless the Lord! The God of our salvation
supports us day after day!"*
—Psalm 68:19

FREEDOM & FORGIVENESS

What am I
struggling with?

*"Be encouraged, my child, your sins are
forgiven."*
—Matthew 9:2

PRAYER PETITIONS

What are my
prayer requests?

*"Don't be anxious about anything; rather, bring
up all your requests to God in your prayers and
petitions, along with giving thanks."*
—Philippians 4:6

MY HEART / MY PASSION

What is going
on with me?

*"We are God's accomplishment, created in
Christ Jesus to do good things.
God planned these good things to be the way
that we live our lives."*
—Ephesians 2:10

AMBASSADOR NOTES

Who did I share
Jesus with today?

*"Preach the word. Be ready to do it whether it
is convenient or inconvenient.
Correct, confront, and encourage with
patience and instruction."*
—2 Timothy 4:2

INSIGHT & UPDATES

What am I seeing God
do with my prayer?

*"What of the wisdom from above?
First, it is pure, and then peaceful, gentle,
obedient, filled with mercy and
good actions, fair and genuine."*
—James 3:17

The end of everything has come. Therefore, be self-controlled and clearheaded so you can pray." —1 Peter 4:7

GOD ANSWERS	AT THE RIGHT TIME	ADDITIONAL NOTES
What is God's answer to my prayer?	When did God answer my prayer?	

"We know that God works all things together for good for the ones who love God, for those who are called according to his purpose."
—Romans 8:28

"Keep alert, because you don't know the day or the hour."
—Matthew 25:13

EARS TO HEAR	FAITH & FOLLOW-THROUGH	ADDITIONAL NOTES
What is God saying to me?	How and when did I respond to God?	

"Focus on working on your own development and on what you teach. If you do this, you will save yourself and those who hear you."
—1 Timothy 4:16

"Much will be demanded from everyone who has been given much, and from the one who has been entrusted with much, even more will be asked."
—Luke 12:48

Week _____

PRAISE & THANKSGIVING

What may I praise and
thank God for today?

*"Bless the Lord! The God of our salvation
supports us day after day!"*
—Psalm 68:19

FREEDOM & FORGIVENESS

What am I
struggling with?

*"Be encouraged, my child, your sins are
forgiven."*
—Matthew 9:2

PRAYER PETITIONS

What are my
prayer requests?

*"Don't be anxious about anything; rather, br
up all your requests to God in your prayers a
petitions, along with giving thanks."*
—Philippians 4:6

_____

_____

_____

_____

_____

_____

_____

_____

_____

_____

MY HEART / MY PASSION

What is going
on with me?

*"We are God's accomplishment, created in
Christ Jesus to do good things.
God planned these good things to be the way
that we live our lives."*
—Ephesians 2:10

AMBASSADOR NOTES

Who did I share
Jesus with today?

*"Preach the word. Be ready to do it whether it
is convenient or inconvenient.
Correct, confront, and encourage with
patience and instruction."*
—2 Timothy 4:2

INSIGHT & UPDATES

What am I seeing God
do with my prayer?

*"What of the wisdom from above?
First, it is pure, and then peaceful, gentle
obedient, filled with mercy and
good actions, fair and genuine."*
—James 3:17

_____

_____

_____

_____

_____

_____

_____

_____

_____

GOD ANSWERS	AT THE RIGHT TIME	ADDITIONAL NOTES
What is God's answer to my prayer?	When did God answer my prayer?	

"We know that God works all things together for good for the ones who love God, for those who are called according to his purpose." —Romans 8:28

"Keep alert, because you don't know the day or the hour." —Matthew 25:13

EARS TO HEAR	FAITH & FOLLOW-THROUGH	ADDITIONAL NOTES
What is God saying to me?	How and when did I respond to God?	

"Focus on working on your own development and on what you teach. If you do this, you will save yourself and those who hear you." —1 Timothy 4:16

"Much will be demanded from everyone who has been given much, and from the one who has been entrusted with much, even more will be asked." —Luke 12:48

Week _____

*"Bless the Lord! The God of our salvation
supports us day after day!"*
—Psalm 68:19

_____
_____
_____
_____
_____
_____
_____
_____
_____
_____

*"Be encouraged, my child, your sins are
forgiven."*
—Matthew 9:2

_____
_____
_____
_____
_____
_____
_____
_____
_____
_____

*"Don't be anxious about anything; rather, br
up all your requests to God in your prayers a
petitions, along with giving thanks."*
—Philippians 4:6

_____
_____
_____
_____
_____
_____
_____
_____
_____

*"We are God's accomplishment, created in
Christ Jesus to do good things.
God planned these good things to be the way
that we live our lives."*
—Ephesians 2:10

_____
_____
_____
_____
_____
_____
_____
_____

*"Preach the word. Be ready to do it whether it
is convenient or inconvenient.
Correct, confront, and encourage with
patience and instruction."*
—2 Timothy 4:2

_____
_____
_____
_____
_____
_____
_____
_____

*"What of the wisdom from above?
First, it is pure, and then peaceful, gentle
obedient, filled with mercy and
good actions, fair and genuine."*
—James 3:17

_____
_____
_____
_____
_____
_____
_____
_____

"The end of everything has come. Therefore, be self-controlled and clearheaded so you can pray." —I Peter 4:7

GOD ANSWERS	AT THE RIGHT TIME	ADDITIONAL NOTES
What is God's answer to my prayer?	When did God answer my prayer?	

"We know that God works all things together for good for the ones who love God, for those who are called according to his purpose."
—Romans 8:28

"Keep alert, because you don't know the day or the hour."
—Matthew 25:13

EARS TO HEAR	FAITH & FOLLOW-THROUGH	ADDITIONAL NOTES
What is God saying to me?	How and when did I respond to God?	

"Focus on working on your own development and on what you teach. If you do this, you will save yourself and those who hear you."
—I Timothy 4:16

"Much will be demanded from everyone who has been given much, and from the one who has been entrusted with much, even more will be asked."
—Luke 12:48

PRAISE & THANKSGIVING

What may I praise and
thank God for today?

"Bless the Lord! The God of our salvation
supports us day after day!"
—Psalm 68:19

_____

_____

_____

_____

_____

_____

_____

_____

_____

_____

FREEDOM & FORGIVENESS

What am I
struggling with?

"Be encouraged, my child, your sins are
forgiven."
—Matthew 9:2

_____

_____

_____

_____

_____

_____

_____

_____

_____

_____

PRAYER PETITIONS

What are my
prayer requests?

"Don't be anxious about anything; rather, bring
up all your requests to God in your prayers and
petitions, along with giving thanks."
—Philippians 4:6

_____

_____

_____

_____

_____

_____

_____

_____

_____

_____

MY HEART / MY PASSION

What is going
on with me?

"We are God's accomplishment, created in
Christ Jesus to do good things.
God planned these good things to be the way
that we live our lives."
—Ephesians 2:10

_____

_____

_____

_____

_____

_____

_____

_____

AMBASSADOR NOTES

Who did I share
Jesus with today?

"Preach the word. Be ready to do it whether it
is convenient or inconvenient.
Correct, confront, and encourage with
patience and instruction."
—2 Timothy 4:2

_____

_____

_____

_____

_____

_____

_____

_____

INSIGHT & UPDATES

What am I seeing God
do with my prayer?

"What of the wisdom from above?
First, it is pure, and then peaceful, gentle,
obedient, filled with mercy and
good actions, fair and genuine."
—James 3:17

_____

_____

_____

_____

_____

_____

_____

_____

"The end of everything has come. Therefore, be self-controlled and clearheaded so you can pray." —I Peter 4:7

GOD ANSWERS	AT THE RIGHT TIME	ADDITIONAL NOTES
What is God's answer to my prayer?	When did God answer my prayer?	

"We know that God works all things together for good for the ones who love God, for those who are called according to his purpose."
—Romans 8:28

"Keep alert, because you don't know the day or the hour."
—Matthew 25:13

EARS TO HEAR	FAITH & FOLLOW-THROUGH	ADDITIONAL NOTES
What is God saying to me?	How and when did I respond to God?	

"Focus on working on your own development and on what you teach. If you do this, you will save yourself and those who hear you."
—I Timothy 4:16

"Much will be demanded from everyone who has been given much, and from the one who has been entrusted with much, even more will be asked."
—Luke 12:48

PRAISE & THANKSGIVING

What may I praise and
thank God for today?

*"The LORD's name is a strong tower; the
righteous run to it and find refuge."*
—Proverbs 18:10

_____

_____

_____

_____

_____

_____

_____

_____

_____

_____

FREEDOM & FORGIVENESS

What am I
struggling with?

*"The commandment is a lamp and instruction
a light; corrective teaching is the path of life."*
—Proverbs 6:23

_____

_____

_____

_____

_____

_____

_____

_____

_____

_____

PRAYER PETITIONS

What are my
prayer requests?

*"Glory to God, who is able to do
far beyond all that we ask or imagine by his
power at work within us."*
—Ephesians 3:20

_____

_____

_____

_____

_____

_____

_____

_____

_____

_____

MY HEART / MY PASSION

What is going
on with me?

*"I'm sure about this: the one who started a
good work in you will stay with you to complete the job by the day of Christ Jesus."*
—Philippians 1:6

_____

_____

_____

_____

_____

_____

_____

_____

_____

AMBASSADOR NOTES

Who did I share
Jesus with today?

*"But you must keep control of yourself in all
circumstances. Endure suffering, do the work
of a preacher of the good news, and carry out
your service fully."*
—2 Timothy 4:5

_____

_____

_____

_____

_____

_____

_____

_____

_____

INSIGHT & UPDATES

What am I seeing God
do with my prayer?

*"The wise hear them and grow in wisdom;
those with understanding gain guidance."*
—Proverbs 1:5

_____

_____

_____

_____

_____

_____

_____

_____

_____

"The end of everything has come. Therefore, be self-controlled and clearheaded so you can pray." —I Peter 4:7

GOD ANSWERS	AT THE RIGHT TIME	ADDITIONAL NOTES
What is God's answer to my prayer?	When did God answer my prayer?	

"Many plans are in a person's mind, but the Lord's purpose will succeed."
—Proverbs 19:21

"Look, now is the right time! Look, now is the day of salvation!"
—2 Corinthians 6:2

EARS TO HEAR	FAITH & FOLLOW-THROUGH	ADDITIONAL NOTES
What is God saying to me?	How and when did I respond to God?	

"Don't withhold good from someone who deserves it, when it is in your power to do so."
—Proverbs 3:27

"Don't say to your neighbor, 'Go and come back; I'll give it to you tomorrow,' when you have it."
—Proverbs 3:28

Week _____

PRAISE & THANKSGIVING

What may I praise and
thank God for today?

*"The LORD's name is a strong tower; the
righteous run to it and find refuge."*
—Proverbs 18:10

_____
_____
_____
_____
_____
_____
_____
_____
_____
_____

FREEDOM & FORGIVENESS

What am I
struggling with?

*"The commandment is a lamp and instruction
a light; corrective teaching is the path of life."*
—Proverbs 6:23

_____
_____
_____
_____
_____
_____
_____
_____
_____
_____

PRAYER PETITIONS

What are my
prayer requests?

*"Glory to God, who is able to do
far beyond all that we ask or imagine by h
power at work within us."*
—Ephesians 3:20

_____
_____
_____
_____
_____
_____
_____
_____
_____

MY HEART / MY PASSION

What is going
on with me?

*"I'm sure about this: the one who started a
good work in you will stay with you to complete the job by the day of Christ Jesus."*
—Philippians 1:6

_____
_____
_____
_____
_____
_____
_____
_____
_____

AMBASSADOR NOTES

Who did I share
Jesus with today?

*"But you must keep control of yourself in all
circumstances. Endure suffering, do the work
of a preacher of the good news, and carry out
your service fully."*
—2 Timothy 4:5

_____
_____
_____
_____
_____
_____
_____
_____
_____

INSIGHT & UPDATES

What am I seeing God
do with my prayer?

*"The wise hear them and grow in wisdom
those with understanding gain guidance."*
—Proverbs 1:5

_____
_____
_____
_____
_____
_____
_____
_____

"The end of everything has come. Therefore, be self-controlled and clearheaded so you can pray." —I Peter 4:7

GOD ANSWERS	AT THE RIGHT TIME	ADDITIONAL NOTES
What is God's answer to my prayer?	When did God answer my prayer?	

"Many plans are in a person's mind, but the Lord's purpose will succeed."
—Proverbs 19:21

"Look, now is the right time! Look, now is the day of salvation!"
—2 Corinthians 6:2

EARS TO HEAR	FAITH & FOLLOW-THROUGH	ADDITIONAL NOTES
What is God saying to me?	How and when did I respond to God?	

"Don't withhold good from someone who deserves it, when it is in your power to do so."
—Proverbs 3:27

"Don't say to your neighbor, 'Go and come back; I'll give it to you tomorrow,' when you have it."
—Proverbs 3:28

PRAISE & THANKSGIVING

What may I praise and
thank God for today?

*"The LORD's name is a strong tower; the
righteous run to it and find refuge."*
—Proverbs 18:10

_____

_____

_____

_____

_____

_____

_____

_____

_____

_____

FREEDOM & FORGIVENESS

What am I
struggling with?

*"The commandment is a lamp and instruction
a light; corrective teaching is the path of life."*
—Proverbs 6:23

_____

_____

_____

_____

_____

_____

_____

_____

_____

_____

PRAYER PETITIONS

What are my
prayer requests?

*"Glory to God, who is able to do
far beyond all that we ask or imagine by his
power at work within us."*
—Ephesians 3:20

_____

_____

_____

_____

_____

_____

_____

_____

_____

_____

MY HEART / MY PASSION

What is going
on with me?

*"I'm sure about this: the one who started a
good work in you will stay with you to complete the job by the day of Christ Jesus."*
—Philippians 1:6

_____

_____

_____

_____

_____

_____

_____

_____

_____

AMBASSADOR NOTES

Who did I share
Jesus with today?

*"But you must keep control of yourself in all
circumstances. Endure suffering, do the work
of a preacher of the good news, and carry out
your service fully."*
—2 Timothy 4:5

_____

_____

_____

_____

_____

_____

_____

_____

_____

INSIGHT & UPDATES

What am I seeing God
do with my prayer?

*"The wise hear them and grow in wisdom;
those with understanding gain guidance."*
—Proverbs 1:5

_____

_____

_____

_____

_____

_____

_____

_____

_____

GOD ANSWERS	AT THE RIGHT TIME	ADDITIONAL NOTES
What is God's answer to my prayer?	When did God answer my prayer?	

"Many plans are in a person's mind, but the LORD's purpose will succeed."
—Proverbs 19:21

"Look, now is the right time! Look, now is the day of salvation!"
—2 Corinthians 6:2

EARS TO HEAR	FAITH & FOLLOW-THROUGH	ADDITIONAL NOTES
What is God saying to me?	How and when did I respond to God?	

"Don't withhold good from someone who deserves it, when it is in your power to do so."
—Proverbs 3:27

"Don't say to your neighbor, 'Go and come back; I'll give it to you tomorrow,' when you have it."
—Proverbs 3:28

PRAISE & THANKSGIVING

What may I praise and
thank God for today?

"The LORD's name is a strong tower; the
righteous run to it and find refuge."
—Proverbs 18:10

_____
_____
_____
_____
_____
_____
_____
_____
_____
_____

FREEDOM & FORGIVENESS

What am I
struggling with?

"The commandment is a lamp and instruction
a light; corrective teaching is the path of life."
—Proverbs 6:23

_____
_____
_____
_____
_____
_____
_____
_____
_____
_____

PRAYER PETITIONS

What are my
prayer requests?

"Glory to God, who is able to do
far beyond all that we ask or imagine by his
power at work within us."
—Ephesians 3:20

_____
_____
_____
_____
_____
_____
_____
_____
_____
_____

MY HEART / MY PASSION

What is going
on with me?

"I'm sure about this: the one who started a
good work in you will stay with you to com-
plete the job by the day of Christ Jesus."
—Philippians 1:6

_____
_____
_____
_____
_____
_____
_____
_____
_____

AMBASSADOR NOTES

Who did I share
Jesus with today?

"But you must keep control of yourself in all
circumstances. Endure suffering, do the work
of a preacher of the good news, and carry out
your service fully."
—2 Timothy 4:5

_____
_____
_____
_____
_____
_____
_____
_____
_____

INSIGHT & UPDATES

What am I seeing God
do with my prayer?

"The wise hear them and grow in wisdom,
those with understanding gain guidance."
—Proverbs 1:5

_____
_____
_____
_____
_____
_____
_____
_____
_____

The end of everything has come. Therefore, be self-controlled and clearheaded so you can pray." —I Peter 4:7

GOD ANSWERS	AT THE RIGHT TIME	ADDITIONAL NOTES
What is God's answer to my prayer?	When did God answer my prayer?	

"Many plans are in a person's mind, but the LORD's *purpose will succeed."* —Proverbs 19:21

"Look, now is the right time! Look, now is the day of salvation!" —2 Corinthians 6:2

EARS TO HEAR	FAITH & FOLLOW-THROUGH	ADDITIONAL NOTES
What is God saying to me?	How and when did I respond to God?	

"Don't withhold good from someone who deserves it, when it is in your power to do so." —Proverbs 3:27

"Don't say to your neighbor, 'Go and come back; I'll give it to you tomorrow,' when you have it." —Proverbs 3:28

Week _____

PRAISE & THANKSGIVING	FREEDOM & FORGIVENESS	PRAYER PETITIONS
What may I praise and thank God for today?	What am I struggling with?	What are my prayer requests?

"The LORD's name is a strong tower; the righteous run to it and find refuge."
—Proverbs 18:10

"The commandment is a lamp and instruction a light; corrective teaching is the path of life."
—Proverbs 6:23

"Glory to God, who is able to do far beyond all that we ask or imagine by his power at work within us."
—Ephesians 3:20

MY HEART / MY PASSION	AMBASSADOR NOTES	INSIGHT & UPDATES
What is going on with me?	Who did I share Jesus with today?	What am I seeing God do with my prayer?

"I'm sure about this: the one who started a good work in you will stay with you to complete the job by the day of Christ Jesus."
—Philippians 1:6

"But you must keep control of yourself in all circumstances. Endure suffering, do the work of a preacher of the good news, and carry out your service fully."
—2 Timothy 4:5

"The wise hear them and grow in wisdom, those with understanding gain guidance."
—Proverbs 1:5

"The end of everything has come. Therefore, be self-controlled and clearheaded so you can pray." —I Peter 4:7

GOD ANSWERS	AT THE RIGHT TIME	ADDITIONAL NOTES
What is God's answer to my prayer?	When did God answer my prayer?	

"Many plans are in a person's mind, but the LORD's purpose will succeed." —Proverbs 19:21

"Look, now is the right time! Look, now is the day of salvation!" —2 Corinthians 6:2

EARS TO HEAR	FAITH & FOLLOW-THROUGH	ADDITIONAL NOTES
What is God saying to me?	How and when did I respond to God?	

"Don't withhold good from someone who deserves it, when it is in your power to do so." —Proverbs 3:27

"Don't say to your neighbor, 'Go and come back; I'll give it to you tomorrow,' when you have it." —Proverbs 3:28

PRAISE & THANKSGIVING

What may I praise and
thank God for today?

*"True devotion, the kind that is
pure and faultless before God the Father,
is this: to care for the orphans and widows
in their difficulties and to keep the
world from contaminating us."*
—James 1:27

FREEDOM & FORGIVENESS

What am I
struggling with?

*"He rescued us from the control of darkness
and transferred us into the kingdom of the
Son he loves."*
—Colossians 1:13

PRAYER PETITIONS

What are my
prayer requests?

*"Keep on praying and guard your prayers
with thanksgiving."*
—Colossians 4:2

MY HEART / MY PASSION

What is going
on with me?

*"The peace of Christ must control your
hearts—a peace into which you were called in
one body. And be thankful people."*
—Colossians 3:15

AMBASSADOR NOTES

Who did I share
Jesus with today?

*"Pray that I might be able to make it as
clear as I ought to when I preach. Act wisely
toward outsiders, making the most of the
opportunity."*
—Colossians 4:4-5

INSIGHT & UPDATES

What am I seeing God
do with my prayer?

*"Since the day we heard about you, we haven't
stopped praying for you and asking for you to
be filled with the knowledge of God's will, with
all wisdom and spiritual understanding."*
—Colossians 1:9

*The end of everything has come. Therefore, be self-controlled and clearheaded so you can pray." —*I Peter 4:7

GOD ANSWERS	AT THE RIGHT TIME	ADDITIONAL NOTES
What is God's answer to my prayer?	When did God answer my prayer?	

"Take delight in the LORD, and he will give you the desires of your heart."
—Psalm 37:4 NIV

"But if we hope for what we don't see, we wait for it with patience."
—Romans 8:25

EARS TO HEAR	FAITH & FOLLOW-THROUGH	ADDITIONAL NOTES
What is God saying to me?	How and when did I respond to God?	

"Whatever you do, whether in speech or action, do it all in the name of the Lord Jesus and give thanks to God the Father through him."
—Colossians 3:17

"I work hard and struggle for this goal with his energy, which works in me powerfully."
—Colossians 1:29

PRAISE & THANKSGIVING

What may I praise and
thank God for today?

*"True devotion, the kind that is
pure and faultless before God the Father,
is this: to care for the orphans and widows
in their difficulties and to keep the
world from contaminating us."*
—James 1:27

_____

_____

_____

_____

_____

_____

_____

_____

_____

FREEDOM & FORGIVENESS

What am I
struggling with?

*"He rescued us from the control of darkness
and transferred us into the kingdom of the
Son he loves."*
—Colossians 1:13

_____

_____

_____

_____

_____

_____

_____

_____

_____

PRAYER PETITIONS

What are my
prayer requests?

*"Keep on praying and guard your prayers
with thanksgiving."*
—Colossians 4:2

_____

_____

_____

_____

_____

_____

_____

_____

_____

MY HEART / MY PASSION

What is going
on with me?

*"The peace of Christ must control your
hearts—a peace into which you were called in
one body. And be thankful people."*
—Colossians 3:15

_____

_____

_____

_____

_____

_____

_____

_____

AMBASSADOR NOTES

Who did I share
Jesus with today?

*"Pray that I might be able to make it as
clear as I ought to when I preach. Act wisely
toward outsiders, making the most of the
opportunity."*
—Colossians 4:4-5

_____

_____

_____

_____

_____

_____

_____

_____

INSIGHT & UPDATES

What am I seeing God
do with my prayer?

*"Since the day we heard about you, we have
stopped praying for you and asking for you
be filled with the knowledge of God's will, w
all wisdom and spiritual understanding."*
—Colossians 1:9

_____

_____

_____

_____

_____

_____

_____

_____

"The end of everything has come. Therefore, be self-controlled and clearheaded so you can pray." —1 Peter 4:7

GOD ANSWERS	AT THE RIGHT TIME	ADDITIONAL NOTES
What is God's answer to my prayer?	When did God answer my prayer?	

"Take delight in the LORD, and he will give you the desires of your heart."
—Psalm 37:4 NIV

"But if we hope for what we don't see, we wait for it with patience."
—Romans 8:25

EARS TO HEAR	FAITH & FOLLOW-THROUGH	ADDITIONAL NOTES
What is God saying to me?	How and when did I respond to God?	

"Whatever you do, whether in speech or action, do it all in the name of the Lord Jesus and give thanks to God the Father through him."
—Colossians 3:17

"I work hard and struggle for this goal with his energy, which works in me powerfully."
—Colossians 1:29

PRAISE & THANKSGIVING

What may I praise and
thank God for today?

*"True devotion, the kind that is
pure and faultless before God the Father,
is this: to care for the orphans and widows
in their difficulties and to keep the
world from contaminating us."*
—James 1:27

_____
_____
_____
_____
_____
_____
_____
_____
_____

FREEDOM & FORGIVENESS

What am I
struggling with?

*"He rescued us from the control of darkness
and transferred us into the kingdom of the
Son he loves."*
—Colossians 1:13

_____
_____
_____
_____
_____
_____
_____
_____
_____

PRAYER PETITIONS

What are my
prayer requests?

*"Keep on praying and guard your prayers
with thanksgiving."*
—Colossians 4:2

_____
_____
_____
_____
_____
_____
_____
_____
_____

MY HEART / MY PASSION

What is going
on with me?

*"The peace of Christ must control your
hearts—a peace into which you were called in
one body. And be thankful people."*
—Colossians 3:15

_____
_____
_____
_____
_____
_____
_____
_____
_____

AMBASSADOR NOTES

Who did I share
Jesus with today?

*"Pray that I might be able to make it as
clear as I ought to when I preach. Act wisely
toward outsiders, making the most of the
opportunity."*
—Colossians 4:4-5

_____
_____
_____
_____
_____
_____
_____
_____
_____

INSIGHT & UPDATES

What am I seeing God
do with my prayer?

*"Since the day we heard about you, we have
stopped praying for you and asking for you
be filled with the knowledge of God's will, w
all wisdom and spiritual understanding."*
—Colossians 1:9

_____
_____
_____
_____
_____
_____
_____
_____
_____

"The end of everything has come. Therefore, be self-controlled and clearheaded so you can pray." —I Peter 4:7

GOD ANSWERS	AT THE RIGHT TIME	ADDITIONAL NOTES
What is God's answer to my prayer?	When did God answer my prayer?	

"Take delight in the LORD, and he will give you the desires of your heart."
—Psalm 37:4 NIV

"But if we hope for what we don't see, we wait for it with patience."
—Romans 8:25

EARS TO HEAR	FAITH & FOLLOW-THROUGH	ADDITIONAL NOTES
What is God saying to me?	How and when did I respond to God?	

"Whatever you do, whether in speech or action, do it all in the name of the Lord Jesus and give thanks to God the Father through him."
—Colossians 3:17

"I work hard and struggle for this goal with his energy, which works in me powerfully."
—Colossians 1:29

PRAISE & THANKSGIVING

What may I praise and
thank God for today?

*"True devotion, the kind that is
pure and faultless before God the Father,
is this: to care for the orphans and widows
in their difficulties and to keep the
world from contaminating us."*
—James 1:27

_____

_____

_____

_____

_____

_____

_____

_____

_____

FREEDOM & FORGIVENESS

What am I
struggling with?

*"He rescued us from the control of darkness
and transferred us into the kingdom of the
Son he loves."*
—Colossians 1:13

_____

_____

_____

_____

_____

_____

_____

_____

_____

PRAYER PETITIONS

What are my
prayer requests?

*"Keep on praying and guard your prayers
with thanksgiving."*
—Colossians 4:2

_____

_____

_____

_____

_____

_____

_____

_____

_____

MY HEART / MY PASSION

What is going
on with me?

*"The peace of Christ must control your
hearts—a peace into which you were called in
one body. And be thankful people."*
—Colossians 3:15

_____

_____

_____

_____

_____

_____

_____

_____

_____

AMBASSADOR NOTES

Who did I share
Jesus with today?

*"Pray that I might be able to make it as
clear as I ought to when I preach. Act wisely
toward outsiders, making the most of the
opportunity."*
—Colossians 4:4-5

_____

_____

_____

_____

_____

_____

_____

_____

_____

INSIGHT & UPDATES

What am I seeing God
do with my prayer?

*"Since the day we heard about you, we haven't
stopped praying for you and asking for you to
be filled with the knowledge of God's will, with
all wisdom and spiritual understanding."*
—Colossians 1:9

_____

_____

_____

_____

_____

_____

_____

_____

_____

The end of everything has come. Therefore, be self-controlled and clearheaded so you can pray." —I Peter 4:7

GOD ANSWERS	AT THE RIGHT TIME	ADDITIONAL NOTES
What is God's answer to my prayer?	When did God answer my prayer?	

"Take delight in the LORD, and he will give you the desires of your heart."
—Psalm 37:4 NIV

"But if we hope for what we don't see, we wait for it with patience."
—Romans 8:25

EARS TO HEAR	FAITH & FOLLOW-THROUGH	ADDITIONAL NOTES
What is God saying to me?	How and when did I respond to God?	

"Whatever you do, whether in speech or action, do it all in the name of the Lord Jesus and give thanks to God the Father through him."
—Colossians 3:17

"I work hard and struggle for this goal with his energy, which works in me powerfully."
—Colossians 1:29

PRAISE & THANKSGIVING

What may I praise and
thank God for today?

*"True devotion, the kind that is
pure and faultless before God the Father,
is this: to care for the orphans and widows
in their difficulties and to keep the
world from contaminating us."*
—James 1:27

_____

_____

_____

_____

_____

_____

_____

_____

_____

_____

FREEDOM & FORGIVENESS

What am I
struggling with?

*"He rescued us from the control of darkness
and transferred us into the kingdom of the
Son he loves."*
—Colossians 1:13

_____

_____

_____

_____

_____

_____

_____

_____

_____

_____

PRAYER PETITIONS

What are my
prayer requests?

*"Keep on praying and guard your prayer
with thanksgiving."*
—Colossians 4:2

_____

_____

_____

_____

_____

_____

_____

_____

_____

_____

MY HEART / MY PASSION

What is going
on with me?

*"The peace of Christ must control your
hearts—a peace into which you were called in
one body. And be thankful people."*
—Colossians 3:15

_____

_____

_____

_____

_____

_____

_____

_____

_____

AMBASSADOR NOTES

Who did I share
Jesus with today?

*"Pray that I might be able to make it as
clear as I ought to when I preach. Act wisely
toward outsiders, making the most of the
opportunity."*
—Colossians 4:4-5

_____

_____

_____

_____

_____

_____

_____

_____

_____

INSIGHT & UPDATES

What am I seeing God
do with my prayer?

*"Since the day we heard about you, we have
stopped praying for you and asking for you
be filled with the knowledge of God's will, w
all wisdom and spiritual understanding."*
—Colossians 1:9

_____

_____

_____

_____

_____

_____

_____

_____

_____

GOD ANSWERS	AT THE RIGHT TIME	ADDITIONAL NOTES
What is God's answer to my prayer?	When did God answer my prayer?	

"Take delight in the LORD, and he will give you the desires of your heart."
—Psalm 37:4 NIV

"But if we hope for what we don't see, we wait for it with patience."
—Romans 8:25

EARS TO HEAR	FAITH & FOLLOW-THROUGH	ADDITIONAL NOTES
What is God saying to me?	How and when did I respond to God?	

"Whatever you do, whether in speech or action, do it all in the name of the Lord Jesus and give thanks to God the Father through him."
—Colossians 3:17

"I work hard and struggle for this goal with his energy, which works in me powerfully."
—Colossians 1:29

PRAISE & THANKSGIVING

What may I praise and
thank God for today?

*"But I have trusted in your faithful love.
My heart will rejoice in your salvation. Yes,
I will sing to the LORD because he has been
good to me."*
—Psalm 13:5-6

FREEDOM & FORGIVENESS

What am I
struggling with?

*"Save your servant from willful sins. Don't let
them rule me. Then I'll be completely blame-
less; I'll be innocent of great wrongdoing."*
—Psalm 19:13

PRAYER PETITIONS

What are my
prayer requests?

*"What should I do? I'll pray in the Spirit,
I'll pray with my mind too...."*
—I Corinthians 14:15

MY HEART / MY PASSION

What is going
on with me?

*"We have been examined and approved by
God to be trusted with the good news....
We aren't trying to please people, but we
are trying to please God, who continues to
examine our hearts."*
—I Thessalonians 2:4

AMBASSADOR NOTES

Who did I share
Jesus with today?

*"Go and make disciples of all nations, bap-
tizing them in the name of the Father and of
the Son and of the Holy Spirit, teaching them
to obey everything that I've commanded you."*
—Matthew 28:19-20

INSIGHT & UPDATES

What am I seeing God
do with my prayer?

*"Faith is the reality of what we hope for,
proof of what we don't see."*
—Hebrews 11:1

"The end of everything has come. Therefore, be self-controlled and clearheaded so you can pray." —I Peter 4:7

GOD ANSWERS	AT THE RIGHT TIME	ADDITIONAL NOTES
What is God's answer to my prayer?	When did God answer my prayer?	

"Consider God's work!" —Ecclesiastes 7:13

"The LORD is my portion! Therefore, I will wait for him." —Lamentations 3:24

EARS TO HEAR	FAITH & FOLLOW-THROUGH	ADDITIONAL NOTES
What is God saying to me?	How and when did I respond to God?	

"A person's steps are from the LORD." —Proverbs 20:24

"Whoever keeps a command will meet no harm, and the wise heart knows the right time and the right way." —Ecclesiastes 8:5

PRAISE & THANKSGIVING

What may I praise and
thank God for today?

*"But I have trusted in your faithful love.
My heart will rejoice in your salvation. Yes,
I will sing to the Lord because he has been
good to me."*
—Psalm 13:5-6

FREEDOM & FORGIVENESS

What am I
struggling with?

*"Save your servant from willful sins. Don't let
them rule me. Then I'll be completely blame-
less; I'll be innocent of great wrongdoing."*
—Psalm 19:13

PRAYER PETITIONS

What are my
prayer requests?

*"What should I do? I'll pray in the Spirit, bu
I'll pray with my mind too...."*
—1 Corinthians 14:15

MY HEART / MY PASSION

What is going
on with me?

*"We have been examined and approved by
God to be trusted with the good news. . . .
We aren't trying to please people, but we
are trying to please God, who continues to
examine our hearts."*
—1 Thessalonians 2:4

AMBASSADOR NOTES

Who did I share
Jesus with today?

*"Go and make disciples of all nations, bap-
tizing them in the name of the Father and of
the Son and of the Holy Spirit, teaching them
to obey everything that I've commanded you."*
—Matthew 28:19-20

INSIGHT & UPDATES

What am I seeing God
do with my prayer?

*"Faith is the reality of what we hope for, the
proof of what we don't see."*
—Hebrews 11:1

The end of everything has come. Therefore, be self-controlled and clearheaded so you can pray." —I Peter 4:7

GOD ANSWERS	AT THE RIGHT TIME	ADDITIONAL NOTES
What is God's answer to my prayer?	When did God answer my prayer?	

"Consider God's work!"
—Ecclesiastes 7:13

"The LORD is my portion! Therefore, I will wait for him."
—Lamentations 3:24

EARS TO HEAR	FAITH & FOLLOW-THROUGH	ADDITIONAL NOTES
What is God saying to me?	How and when did I respond to God?	

"A person's steps are from the LORD."
—Proverbs 20:24

"Whoever keeps a command will meet no harm, and the wise heart knows the right time and the right way."
—Ecclesiastes 8:5

PRAISE & THANKSGIVING

What may I praise and
thank God for today?

*"But I have trusted in your faithful love.
My heart will rejoice in your salvation. Yes,
I will sing to the LORD because he has been
good to me."*
—Psalm 13:5-6

_____

_____

_____

_____

_____

_____

_____

_____

_____

FREEDOM & FORGIVENESS

What am I
struggling with?

*"Save your servant from willful sins. Don't let
them rule me. Then I'll be completely blame-
less; I'll be innocent of great wrongdoing."*
—Psalm 19:13

_____

_____

_____

_____

_____

_____

_____

_____

_____

PRAYER PETITIONS

What are my
prayer requests?

*"What should I do? I'll pray in the Spirit, b
I'll pray with my mind too...."*
—I Corinthians 14:15

_____

_____

_____

_____

_____

_____

_____

_____

_____

MY HEART / MY PASSION

What is going
on with me?

*"We have been examined and approved by
God to be trusted with the good news. . . .
We aren't trying to please people, but we
are trying to please God, who continues to
examine our hearts."*
—I Thessalonians 2:4

_____

_____

_____

_____

_____

_____

_____

_____

_____

AMBASSADOR NOTES

Who did I share
Jesus with today?

*"Go and make disciples of all nations, bap-
tizing them in the name of the Father and of
the Son and of the Holy Spirit, teaching them
to obey everything that I've commanded you."*
—Matthew 28:19-20

_____

_____

_____

_____

_____

_____

_____

_____

_____

INSIGHT & UPDATES

What am I seeing God
do with my prayer?

*"Faith is the reality of what we hope for, th
proof of what we don't see."*
—Hebrews 11:1

_____

_____

_____

_____

_____

_____

_____

_____

_____

The end of everything has come. Therefore, be self-controlled and clearheaded so you can pray." —I Peter 4:7

GOD ANSWERS	AT THE RIGHT TIME	ADDITIONAL NOTES
What is God's answer to my prayer?	When did God answer my prayer?	

"Consider God's work!"
—Ecclesiastes 7:13

"The LORD is my portion! Therefore, I will wait for him."
—Lamentations 3:24

EARS TO HEAR	FAITH & FOLLOW-THROUGH	ADDITIONAL NOTES
What is God saying to me?	How and when did I respond to God?	

"A person's steps are from the LORD."
—Proverbs 20:24

"Whoever keeps a command will meet no harm, and the wise heart knows the right time and the right way."
—Ecclesiastes 8:5

PRAISE & THANKSGIVING

What may I praise and
thank God for today?

"But I have trusted in your faithful love.
My heart will rejoice in your salvation. Yes,
I will sing to the LORD because he has been
good to me."
—Psalm 13:5-6

_____
_____
_____
_____
_____
_____
_____
_____
_____
_____

FREEDOM & FORGIVENESS

What am I
struggling with?

"Save your servant from willful sins. Don't let
them rule me. Then I'll be completely blame-
less; I'll be innocent of great wrongdoing."
—Psalm 19:13

_____
_____
_____
_____
_____
_____
_____
_____
_____
_____

PRAYER PETITIONS

What are my
prayer requests?

"What should I do? I'll pray in the Spirit,
I'll pray with my mind too...."
—1 Corinthians 14:15

_____
_____
_____
_____
_____
_____
_____
_____
_____
_____

MY HEART / MY PASSION

What is going
on with me?

"We have been examined and approved by
God to be trusted with the good news. . . .
We aren't trying to please people, but we
are trying to please God, who continues to
examine our hearts."
—1 Thessalonians 2:4

_____
_____
_____
_____
_____
_____
_____
_____
_____

AMBASSADOR NOTES

Who did I share
Jesus with today?

"Go and make disciples of all nations, bap-
tizing them in the name of the Father and of
the Son and of the Holy Spirit, teaching them
to obey everything that I've commanded you."
—Matthew 28:19-20

_____
_____
_____
_____
_____
_____
_____
_____
_____

INSIGHT & UPDATES

What am I seeing God
do with my prayer?

"Faith is the reality of what we hope for,
proof of what we don't see."
—Hebrews 11:1

_____
_____
_____
_____
_____
_____
_____
_____
_____

GOD ANSWERS	AT THE RIGHT TIME	ADDITIONAL NOTES
What is God's answer to my prayer?	When did God answer my prayer?	

"Consider God's work!"
—Ecclesiastes 7:13

"The LORD is my portion! Therefore, I will wait for him."
—Lamentations 3:24

EARS TO HEAR	FAITH & FOLLOW-THROUGH	ADDITIONAL NOTES
What is God saying to me?	How and when did I respond to God?	

"A person's steps are from the LORD."
—Proverbs 20:24

"Whoever keeps a command will meet no harm, and the wise heart knows the right time and the right way."
—Ecclesiastes 8:5